STRANGE TALENTS

MARVELS & MYSTERIES

STRANGE TALENTS

•PARRALLEL•

This material has previously appeared in
partwork form as *The Unexplained*

Published in 1995 by Parrallel
Unit 13-17 Avonbridge Trading Estate,
Atlantic Road, Avonmouth, Bristol BS11 9QD

ISBN 0-75251-207-2

Printed and bound in Singapore

CONTENTS

INTRODUCTION

All the articles in this book are about ordinary people with some extraordinary powers. In some cases, these abilities were developed through hard work, in others they were inborn, or suddenly manifested themselves as the result of an injury or some important event. Some of them may be fakes and fraudsters, some of them are indubitably sincere. Some of them have put their gifts to use for their personal gain, or for the general good; others have talents that are doubly strange, in that they are both inexplicable and fairly useless. Ted Serios, for instance, seems to be able to create images on photographic film using mind power alone, but what does he get out of this very specialized gift for telekinesis? And how did he discover that he had it?

Serios's gift is unique, but other abilities here seem to be shared. Telepathy, telekinesis – the ability to move objects without touching them – intuitive hunches and the power to heal seem, in some degree, to be within the capacity of many people. It appears that they can even be learned, or at least a nascent gift can be trained and developed through working at it.

None of us ever use more than a small percentage of the total capacity of our brains, and it is tempting to think that the bizarre and wonderful abilities demonstrated in this book could be locked away inside all of us, just waiting for the right extraordinary circumstances or the correct training to suddenly burst forth. Because of this there are, among the tales of wonders and accounts of gifted men and women, articles that challenge you to think about your own experiences and potential.

CAN PEOPLE REALLY BE
BURIED ALIVE AND SURVIVE,
OR WITHSTAND FREEZING
TEMPERATURES? IS IT
POSSIBLE TO DEMOLISH A
PILE OF BRICKS WITH JUST A
HAND? THERE IS EVIDENCE
THAT THE ASTOUNDING
POWER OF THE MIND CAN BE
USED TO PUSH THE HUMAN
BODY TO NEW LIMITS

EVERY MAN A SUPERMAN

It can give you the strength to demolish a pile of bricks, the means to kill people without touching them, the ability to raise your sports performance to new heights or the will to regain your health: it is the formidable power of the mind. Over recent years, research has shown that the mind-body relationship, or 'psychosomatic link' as medicine calls it, is deeper and more active than once realised in the West. Indeed, studies of

In a peaceful application of a deadly martial art, karate is used, above, to demolish a building.

Meditation, as demonstrated in an eastern setting, below, is a discipline recognised as effective against stress and in attaining new spiritual heights.

meditation, deep relaxation and other forms of mind-expansion have yielded new information that is helping us towards greater understanding of this mind and body inter-relationship. It is a slow process of exploration, however. We in the West still have no commonly accepted definitions of mind and consciousness, and no philosophical basis for beliefs about their interplay. Small wonder, then, that science has often felt uneasy, not to say downright uncomfortable, when confronted with reports or even actual demonstrations of some of the mind's more spectacular feats.

Dr James Braid, a Scottish ophthalmic surgeon, ran into just such scientific bias in the 1840s when he suggested that people could undergo painless surgery, and proposed the use of hypnosis. His medical colleagues scoffed and sneered: this was, after all, prior to the discovery of anaesthesia. And even after hypnosis had been successfully used over a considerable period of time, many doctors

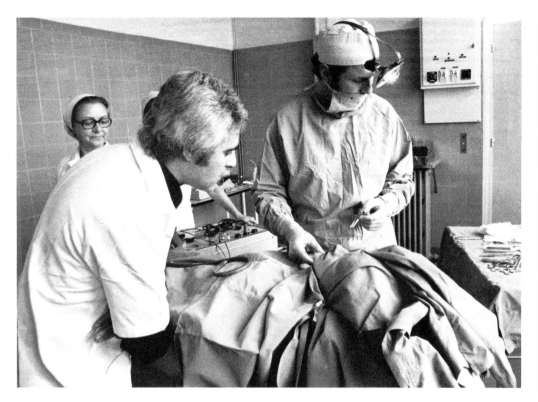

simply refused to believe it was possible to control pain through the mind. But hypnotism is by no means the only condition under which the mind can induce physical changes, as certain discoveries have since shown.

Western scientists have now investigated and validated many claims made for meditation and other Eastern disciplines, even measuring the extent to which disciples can control heart rate and other autonomic functions, for example. And, not unexpectedly, scientific proof of such control actually adds to the amazement inspired by some such feats, as we begin to see how far the human body can be pushed. In order to show how finely they are able to regulate their autonomic functions, for instance, some yogis have stayed buried alive in airtight boxes for a period of days. While anyone else would have suffocated within hours, they managed to eke out the available air supply by reducing their heart rate and breathing to a barely detectable tick-over level. Such a level of control is gained only after years – and sometimes nearly a lifetime – of disciplined training.

INTERNAL FIRE

The Tibetan practice of *tumo* is another source of wonderment. The goal is to allow disciples to withstand the intense cold of their climate, and training includes a long programme of meditation and breathing exercises. Part of this training involves the visualisation of an internal fire as the only source of warmth during meditation in the icy Tibetan climes. How effectively this art of self-heating internally has been mastered is tested in the most demanding way.

On a given cold and windy night, each student is draped in a sheet that has been soaked in icy water. The initiate is required to dry out this sheet with his own body heat, not once but three times in succession. After this test, the final one of the training, the

adept wears nothing more than a single cotton garment, regardless of the season or the harshness of the conditions.

Superhuman prowess is also associated with many of the schools of Eastern martial arts, which cultivate the same kind of self-awareness and self-mastery as religious and spiritual schools. The principle object of martial arts is to enable practitioners to perform feats of strength and acts of combat beyond ordinary limits. According to some accounts, martial arts training creates the ability to tap into some secret power source. But this energy source is seen as accessible to everyone through techniques of training that aim to unify the mind and body. The Japanese call this extraordinary energy *ki*.

A surgeon, above, operates on a hypnotised patient while the hypnotist looks on. The mind-over-body technique of hypnotism has today gained widespread respectability among many orthodox doctors.

A group of Japanese Buddhists, below, pour icy water over themselves in the bitter cold of a Tokyo winter. Mental training enables them to do this without any visible signs of ill effect.

spiritual power or soul power lies within a human body'. Such demonstrations of strength might appear pointless to many, but the karate expert's demolition of a pile of bricks cannot but impress.

The mind can even kill while a person under attack remains untouched, working its own lethal effect so that people quite literally think or worry themselves to death. This direct effect can be clearly seen in the placing of a curse; for in cultures where witchcraft is practised, a curse is almost always effective because the victim believes so strongly in the magic being worked.

In dismissing beliefs of this kind as mere superstition, the sophisticated Westerner overlooks the most important lesson implicit in witchcraft: namely, that suggestion, thought and imagination are unquestionably powerful weapons. But if they can be used to kill, can they not be used to produce beneficial effects?

POSITIVE THINKING

Emile Coué, a French psychotherapist, was convinced that people could make themselves better by simply exerting their minds, and so advised patients to say every morning: 'Every day, in every way, I am getting better and better'. His theories enjoyed a vogue in the 1920s, and his methods can be seen as a forerunner of the visualisation and positive thinking techniques used today by those healers who try to tap the power of the mind in order to aid recovery from illness.

Such new approaches have also been used with some success in the fight against diseases such as cancer; and among the techniques used are relaxation and visualisation exercises designed to help individuals mobilise their resources to conquer their condition.

It is difficult, if not impossible, to identify objectively those changes that result from mental techniques. A notable exception, though, is deep relaxation. A great deal of research has been carried out into transcendental meditation (TM), Zen and other meditation practices in several countries; and studies have shown that the definite, measurable

Methods for developing ki may differ in detail, but in general they all have in common the five elements of relaxation, concentration, breathing exercises, emptying the mind of thought, and rhythmic activity. Some teachers say that there are three stages towards mastery of the energy *ki*. In the first stage, the individual achieves a centralisation of *ki*. In the second, the influence of the energy can reach out beyond one individual to touch others. Then, in the final stage, the master gets in touch with what is believed to be the very centre of life – a stage rarely reached by anyone.

In his film **Enter the Dragon, Bruce Lee smashes an enemy with a kung fu** *blow.* **Kung fu** *is one of many martial arts that develop physical powers through mental training.*

KUNG FU MASTERS

As more and more is written on the martial arts, many stories of paranormal feats come to light. Some of these have been witnessed by observers who testify to their truth. In a public demonstration, Bruce Lee – *kung fu* master and international film star – showed remarkable powers that went nearly beyond the believable. Standing with his right foot forward and his right arm almost fully extended to within an inch (2.5 centimetres) of a man, he struck. Yet, though it is generally accepted that it is physically impossible to generate enough power to hurt someone from this position, Lee sent the man flying.

Moreshei Uyeshiba, founder of *aikido,* is reputed to successfully have moved a boulder that had defeated the efforts of 10 labourers. Explaining this and similar feats, he said: 'I taught myself that an extraordinary

IRON IN THE SOUL

There are many stories of superhuman feats in sports – of achievements that go way beyond the physical prowess achieved by exercise and practice, and that instead are put down to unexplained forces. So far, no systematic study of the paranormal in sports has been made, but there is mounting evidence that success is often due to psychological factors and maybe more. Famous golf professionals in particular often talk about the importance of 'will' in helping them win. It was once said of Arnold Palmer that 'more than anything else, you get the feeling that he actually willed the ball into the hole'. In his book on the game, American golfer Johnny Miller also wrote about Bobby Nichols' special ability to come through in the crunch. Describing a contest between himself and Nichols, he said: 'When he hit the ball, I thought to myself, "There's no way that ball will get to the hole". It was going so slowly, it looked as if it would be a foot [30 centimetres] short. Then I heard Bobby say, "Get in", and it did'.

Jack Nicklaus is also credited with special powers of will. Many observers felt that he could win 'whenever he wanted to', one going so far as to say he 'could will the ball into the cup if he needed a birdie at the 18th'. Can these consistent winners have powers of PK? Until further study is done, nobody can say at this point – but players themselves often seem to feel that there is something quite outside the ordinary that affects the way a game sometimes goes.

changes occurring during meditation can have tremendous therapeutic value. In general, such measurable physiological alterations are associated with the autonomic life support functions that lie beyond normal conscious control.

NATURAL ANTIDOTE

Some researchers believe that meditation offers a natural antidote to the stresses and strains of everyday life because it gives the body a chance to dissipate unwanted build-up of effects resulting from the fight-or-flight response. This response was identified in the 1950s as a legacy from the distant past when our ancestors faced dangers calling for rapid, spontaneous action. Self-preservation dictated that – under threat – people either turn tail and run or stand the ground and fight. Either way, the body needs to gear itself up to unleash the necessary energy. In the Western world, running or fighting is unnecessary except in the most extreme circumstances. But the body does not discriminate between the threat posed by, say, an unjust tax demand or a car heading for a collision. They are threats of a different dimension, but they trigger the same kind of response. And the constant physiological process of keying up, without the release of physical reaction, can take its toll.

Meditation provides what has been dubbed the 'relaxation response' by Dr Herbert Benson of the Harvard Medical School. This relaxation response is a quietening down of pulse rate, blood pressure and other physiological regulators. Once the body has been calmed, the mind can purposefully counteract the adverse effects of the fight-or-light response.

One of the more revolutionary developments growing out of the study of meditation is biofeedback. Its purpose is to make people conscious of physiological functions (of which they are not usually aware) through machines that monitor these

Effigies, such as the one above, are sometimes used to harm a victim by witchcraft. Here a pin has been passed through the doll's mouth with the intention that the victim will be hurt in her mouth, too. The mind, it is believed by some, can be used to kill in this way.

Like the eastern adept, seen right, we can all, it seems, learn to control bodily functions such as heart rate, through the technique of biofeedback.

internal processes and give visual or auditory signals of changes. The theory is that it will then be possible for the individual to control those physiological processes associated with psychological states such as breathing and heart rate. Biofeedback is particularly useful for those who want to reduce high levels of stress or deal with 'blocks' – caused, for instance, by pre-exam anxiety.

MASTERING CONTROL

Once you have been connected to a machine that records the heart rate, the speed of the beat will produce a specific sound tone, heard through a pair of headphones. As you relax, slowing down the heart, you can hear the tone and pitch fall. By concentrating on something calming, you can bring your heart rate down to an acceptable level.

Biofeedback can also help reduce brain activity, inducing a feeling of relaxed – almost meditative – well-being. Electrodes placed on the scalp are connected to an electro-encephalograph (EEG) machine, which detects electrical activity in the brain. As you relax, the normal functioning of the brain slows down and the EEG machine begins to reflect a pattern of so-called 'alpha waves' coming from the cortex (the outer layer of the brain). Knowing when the brain is putting out alpha rhythms will allow you to control thoughts that produce alpha activity, thereby producing greater peace of mind.

Maxwell Cade, an expert on biofeedback and who described his work in *The Awakened Mind*, is a scientist who was also trained in Zen and who has carried our research in the field of healing, as well as self-healing. Biofeedback, he has said, provides a quicker route towards self-awareness and the technique has therapeutic value as well. Biofeedback, Cade claims, is as effective as hypnotherapy in producing 'almost miraculous relief of symptoms' but gives more lasting results. Indeed,

there is clinical evidence that those with hypertension (high blood pressure) can be taught to relax and thereby relieve their condition by watching a machine that gives continuous visual feedback.

Arguably, the preventive and therapeutic aspects of techniques such as meditation, self-help, biofeedback and similar practices are sufficient to command much wider interest among the medical community. But it is in other areas, most especially sport, that their potential has been most avidly seized on, and nowhere more enthusiastically than in Eastern Europe.

Here, a branch of applied psychology, called psychic self-regulation (PSR), has developed. It is a blend of hypnosis, yoga and the martial arts, leading to control of various physiological and psychological functions. Some athletic training programmes, for instance, specifically include meditation, hypnosis and other related techniques.

MENTAL TRAINING

Although the United States has not in general embraced such techniques, the United States Olympic Committee has included biofeedback and mental training courses in some of their programmes. In baseball, the Detroit Tigers are known to have used biofeedback, and the Philadelphia Phillies have tried TM.

Many individual competitors, meanwhile, have used mental techniques to help themselves perform better, among them tennis star Billie Jean King, Olympic 400-metres champion Lee Evans, bodybuilder Arnold Schwarzenegger, and high jumper Dwight Stone. They visualise themselves in advance in the winning position, playing the perfect stroke or extracting the maximum effort. We do not

Arnold Schwarzenegger, right, world-famous bodybuilder and film star, is one of the few Westerners to use mental techniques in training and performing. In contrast, most athletes from the East receive psychological as well as physical training.

yet fully understand how mental techniques actually help to improve sports performance or conquer disease. But there is no reason why people should not expose themselves to mind-over-body systems. It is a generally known that most of us live well below our physical and mental potential. So there certainly seems to be a case for considering those techniques that might stretch us to reach new levels of self-awareness and ability.

RELAXATION FOR MIND AND BODY

Meditation has become increasingly popular in the West in recent years, both as a way to cope with the stresses of daily life and as a medical treatment. The many techniques all have in common the attainment of a deep

An experienced meditator can choose any quiet place to meditate, indoors or out. Many prefer to sit in a yoga posture, such as the 'lotus', shown above.

relaxation – almost suspension – of the mind and body. The following is just one method:

First, find a comfortable seat in a quiet room where you will not be disturbed for at least 15 minutes. It is best to keep your feet flat on the floor and your hands clasped loosely in your lap. Wear something loose.

Now close your eyes and relax your body completely. Do this gradually, starting with the toes and working up little by little to the top of the head.

Breathe in and out of the nose, concentrating until respiration becomes soft, smooth and regular. If your mind begins to wander, pull it back to your breathing.

Empty your mind of all thought. One way to do this is to direct your mind to a spot on your own body, and keep it there. Your breathing will soon become almost imperceptible. Aim to remain in this relaxed state for between 15 and 20 minutes.

Open your eyes gently and come out of the relaxed state very slowly. Enjoy the peaceful feeling that should now have been induced for a few minutes before standing up. Then stretch slowly from head to toe.

PERSPECTIVES

TESTING TELEPATHY

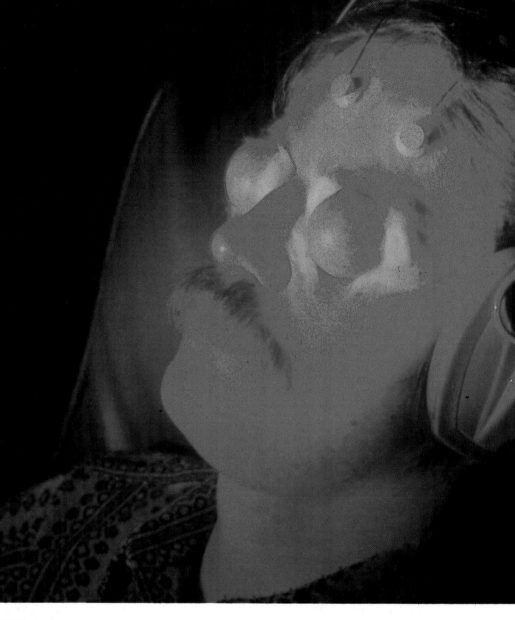

SOME OF US, IT SEEMS, ARE ABLE TO READ THE THOUGHTS OF OTHERS. SCIENCE, HOWEVER, STILL CANNOT EXPLAIN THIS MYSTERIOUS 'TUNING IN'

Early one morning in 1980, a very frightened old lady walked feebly into a Barcelona police station. Senora Isabel Casas, an 81 year-old widow, had been so scared by a terrible dream that, despite her age and infirmity, she had managed to walk to the local police station to raise the alarm. Almost incoherent with fear, she told the officer on duty that she had seen the familiar face of her friend and neighbour, Rafael Perez, 'twisted in terror', and had heard a voice saying: 'they are going to kill us'.

The Spanish police were inclined to dismiss Senora Casas' experience as a mere nightmare. But they became curious when they learned that she had not seen Perez, the only other resident in the block of flats where she lived, for 10 days. Normally, the 56 year-old chef called by every day, but he had written her a note saying he was going away for several weeks. It was odd, the police thought, that this note had not been delivered until three days after she had last seen her neighbour. Why had Perez not called to see her personally?

They decided to investigate, and eventually found Perez tied up in a shed on the roof of the block of flats. He told them that two men had broken into his apartment, made him sign 28 cheques so that they could draw his £15,000 life savings, a

little at a time, and forced him to write the letter to Senora Casas so that her suspicions would not be aroused. Then they tied him up, saying they would be back, once they had all the money, to kill him and his neighbour.

Astonishingly, the old woman seems to have picked up the thoughts of her friend as he waited in terror for his captors to return. His life had been saved by her vivid telepathic dream. The police then ambushed and arrested the men when they returned to the scene of their crime.

This ability of one person to 'look into' the mind of another was one of the first subjects studied by early psychical researchers a century or so ago.

THE CASE OF CANON WARBURTON

Typical of the spontaneous cases of telepathy investigated by these early researchers was the experience of an English clergyman in 1883. Canon Warburton was seated in an armchair in his brother's flat when he began to doze. Suddenly, he woke with a start, and exclaimed 'By Jove! He's down!' The canon had just had a vivid dream in which he had seen his brother come out of a drawing room on to a brightly illuminated landing, catch his foot on the edge of the top stair and fall headlong, only just managing to save himself from serious injury by

using his hands and elbows. The house in the dream was not one that he recognised. All the canon knew, having just arrived in London from Oxford, was that his brother had left him a note explaining that he had gone to a dance in the West End and would be back about 1 a.m.

Recovering from the experience, Canon Warburton then dozed off again, until his brother eventually came in and woke him. 'I have just had as narrow an escape of breaking my neck as I ever had in my life!' he exclaimed. 'Coming out of the ballroom, I caught my foot, and tumbled full length down the stairs.'

This uncanny dream experience is just one of many hundreds of equally impressive cases collected by the Society for Psychical Research in both Britain and America.

CONTROLLED EXPERIMENTS

The word 'telepathy' was originally coined in 1882 by a leading Cambridge scholar and investigator, F.W.H Myers; and the first major study of such experiences – the *Census of Hallucinations*, published in 1890 – examined replies to 20,000 questionnaires. But science needed to examine telepathy under more controlled conditions.

Sir William Barrett, pioneer of scientific research into telepathy and professor of physics at the Royal College of Science, Dublin, conducted a large number of experiments in this area, and finally became satisfied that telepathy was real.

When he first submitted his paper – *Some Phenomena associated with Abnormal Conditions*

of the Mind – to the British Association for the Advancement of Science, however, it was refused by the biological committee. But it was eventually accepted by the anthropological sub-section on the casting vote of its chairman, Dr Alfred Russell Wallace, who was also a keen investigator of psychical phenomena.

By the early part of this century, many groups of researchers were involved in imaginative telepathy tests. In the 1920s, for example, René Warcollier conducted group telepathy experiments between France and the United States, many of which produced very impressive results. But not all early research is acceptable by today's strict scientific standards. The famous physicist Oliver Lodge, for example had carried out tests with two girls who claimed to be able to read each other's minds. He found their demonstrations convincing, and described them in his book *The Survival of Man*, published in 1909. But since the girls were allowed to hold hands while 'sending' telepathic images of playing cards, the possibility that they were using a code cannot be eliminated. This suspicion is reinforced by Lodge's statistics, which show that, when the girls were not touching, results dropped to almost chance level.

TELEPATHIC PICTURES

During the 1930s, the work of writer Upton Sinclair caught public imagination quite strongly. His wife had considerable psychic abilities and was able to 'receive' by telepathy pictures that were drawn by her husband or other senders. Sometimes their

Psychic powers – and telepathy in particular – are known to become heightened during dream states. This, it has been found, can be echoed in a laboratory setting through Ganzfeld (German for 'whole field') experiments. The subject, shown above, relaxes in a darkened room with a dim red light, halved ping-pong balls covering his eyes, and headphones providing white noise. The aim is then to focus on any images that enter the mind while, elsewhere, a 'sender' concentrates hard and tries to communicate.

PERSPECTIVES

IN THE MIND'S EYE

The most impressive scorer in a series of telepathy experiments carried out at Cambridge University by Dr Carl Sargent was Hugh Ashton, who worked with computers by day and played in a punk rock group at night. During one session in 1979, for example, he produced the following taped comments, which are a sample only of the total transcript:

'Buildings in corner. Picture is longer than high. Postcard...concrete, urban, town. Perhaps in Cambridge. Keep thinking of firemen and fire station... Officialdom. Uniforms...Firemen definitely seen. Black and white... People but not face...

'I think one face at bottom in foreground...Policemen's helmet or hat. Facing...smiling...All wearing same uniform...

"Wet, rainy day...White silvery badge on helmet of him looking towards us...Shot looking down..."

The actual target picture, reproduced here, was of firemen taking part in a fire-drill practice in Cambridge. Any comment on the accuracy of Ashton's description would be superfluous, but especially striking have to be the one face turned towards us (all the rest are facing away), the silvery badge on the helmet, and the firemen, who are all wearing the same uniform.

experiments were carried out in adjoining rooms; at other times, over long distances. The results were published in Sinclair's book *Mental Radio,* and reveal that, in 290 experiments, Mrs Sinclair scored 23 per cent successes, 53 per cent partial successes and 24 per cent failures.

The similarity between the original drawings and Mrs Sinclair's 'copies' were often striking, ruling out coincidence but making statistical analysis of the results difficult. In fact, partial successes were often as impressive as direct hits because they provided fascinating insight into how Mrs Sinclair perceived the images. On one occasion, Upton Sinclair drew a volcano with billowing black smoke. His wife drew a very good likeness, but was unable to say what it was, and suggested a beetle. Had this been a telepathy test which required a verbal response, her description of a beetle would have been judged a miss. But her actual drawing showed that she had in fact picked up the image with extraordinary accuracy.

Sinclair, a committed socialist, was well aware that most intelligent people still regarded the phenomenon of telepathy with scepticism. Indeed, some of his socialist friends felt that his interest in ESP conflicted with their rationalist outlook on the world. One of them even attacked him in a newspaper article headed 'Sinclair goes spooky'.

It was to give the subject respectability in the eyes of science that the American Dr J B Rhine began to research in the laboratory, using new methods and easily identifiable targets to ensure there was no doubt whether a subject was scoring a hit or a miss. The results were impressive and satisfied Rhine, as well as many other scientists, that mind-to-mind communication was real.

SCEPTICS

But there were still sceptics, one of whom was the psychologist Bernard Riess. Once, when Dr Rhine was invited to lecture on ESP at Barnard College, Riess questioned him so fiercely that Rhine protested he was, in effect, accusing him of lying. Instead of going on to defend his experiments, however, Rhine suggested to Riess that he should carry out his own tests, using any controls he believed necessary. Riess' students urged him to accept the challenge, and they found a young woman with supposed psychic abilities who agreed to act as a subject. For several months, Riess conducted his own card-guessing experiments with her. Seventy-four runs of 25 cards were made (1,850 trials), and they averaged a phenomenal 18 hits out of 25.

Riess, once a denigrator of ESP research, was then called upon to defend his own experiments in 1938, when the American Psychological Association organised an ESP symposium.

'There can be no criticism of the method used. I had the deck of cards on my desk, shuffled them, and at the stated time turned them over one by one, making a record of each card. I kept the records locked up in my desk and sometimes it was a week before I totalled up the scores and found the number of high scores she was making... The only error that may have crept in is a possibility of deception, and the only person who could have done the deceiving was myself since the subject at

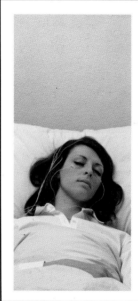

no time knew how well she was doing nor had any idea of which cards were being turned over by myself...' he told the meeting.

ESP-IONAGE!

Rhine's work continued to be a subject of public debate for many years; but with more and more investigators carrying out their own research programmes into various ESP subjects, telepathy was soon overshadowed by such phenomena as clairvoyance and precognition, which brought startling experimental results. Then, in the late 1950s, telepathy was suddenly back in the news with the publication in the French press of reports that successful telepathy tests had been carried out between a submerged American submarine, *USS Nautilus,* and an agent on shore. The possible military implications of such methods of communica-

tion, if they could actually be proved reliable, were obvious.

Despite the United States Navy's denial of the Nautilus story, however, the Soviets took it seriously, with the result that the work of Russian psychical investigators, which had been classed as top secret for 30 years, was at last made public. Among these investigators was Dr Leonid Vasiliev, who claimed that Soviet parapsychologists had received encouragement for their research from high up in the party organisation. Indeed, it is thought that Stalin himself may have been interested in the use of telepathy for military purposes.

TELEPATHIC ORDERS

Dr Vasiliev had been using hypnotised subjects to investigate 'mental radio'; and when a book about this work was published in 1962, he revealed that he and other researchers had been able to make certain individuals carry out instructions by telepathic order. He even claimed to be able to hypnotise by telepathy. In one extraordinary case, a woman whose body was paralysed down the left side was the subject of experiments. Her condition was psychosomatic, however, and without physical cause. Vasiliev discovered that he had only to give mental

*The nuclear submarine USS Nautilus, shown **top**, was rumoured to have been carrying out telepathy experiments between an agent on shore and a sender aboard the submerged craft during the late 1950s. Karl Nikolaiev and Dr Yuri Kamensky, **above left** and **second from right**, took part in a number of experiments involving the sending of Morse messages telepathically.*

*Dr Leonid Vasiliev, the Soviet psychical researcher who used hypnosis to enhance telepathy experiments, is shown **left**.*

commands and she would be able to move her left hand, arm or foot as requested, even without the use of hypnotism.

Demonstrating this form of mental communication before a group of observers as an extra precaution, he blindfolded the subject and did not speak a word. Instead, each instruction was written down and witnessed by the group before either Vasiliev or his co-worker, hypnotist Dr Finne, began concentration. The woman obeyed with remarkable accuracy, and was even able to say whether it was Vasiliev or Finne giving the instruction.

More recently, Russian researchers have carried out even more startling demonstrations of telepathy using a biophysicist, Yuri Kamensky, and an actor and journalist, Karl Nikolaiev. Kamensky was in Novosibirsk in Siberia; Nikolaiev, in Moscow – and a committee of scientists supervised the session.

The results provided overwhelming evidence for mental communication.

In one test, Nikolaiev correctly described six objects that had been given to Kamensky, and was also able to identify 12 out of 20 ESP test cards. What is particularly impressive about these Russian tests, however, is that the scientists succeeded in producing independent instrumental confirmation that something paranormal was going on.

They wired Nikolaiev to an electro-encephalograph (EEG) machine which monitors brain waves. As soon as Kamensky began to transmit images, they found that his brain waves altered. Using this knowledge, they then devised a technique for sending messages in Morse code. Instead of asking Kamensky to think of an object, they asked him to imagine he was fighting Nikolaiev. As the scientists in Moscow watched the recording of Nikolaiev's brain waves on the EEG, they found there was a distinct change in the pattern whenever Kamensky imagined he was fighting him. Kamensky was able to transmit Morse 'dots' and 'dashes' by imagining 'fighting bouts' of various lengths: a 45-second bout produced a burst of activity that was interpreted as a dash, while a 15-second bout was read as a dot. In this way, the scientists in Moscow found they were able to identify the Russian word *mig* – meaning 'instant' – which Kamensky had transmitted in Morse code from as far as 2,000 miles (3,200 kilometres) away in Siberia.

Interestingly, a similar technique using different methods followed the accidental discovery by a Czechoslovakian researcher, Dr Stepan Figar, that intense thought about a person produced an increase in that individual's blood volume – a change that could be accurately measured by a device called a plethysmograph.

MENTAL RADIO

Douglas Dean, a British-born electrochemist and professor of computing, and a leading psychical researcher, saw the potential of this discovery for telepathy tests. His research revealed that, when a telepathic sender concentrates on the name of someone with whom a subject – wired to a plethysmograph – has an emotional tie, a change in the subject's blood volume is often recorded. Together with two engineers from the Newark College of Engineering in New Jersey, Dean went on to design a system using a plethysmograph for sending messages in Morse code.

Its mode of operation is an intriguing one. If the sender concentrates on the name of a person who is emotionally significant to the subject, the plethysmograph produces a measurable response which is interpreted as a Morse dot. If no response is registered during a specified time, however, this is noted as a Morse dash. Using this technique, Dean managed to send a telepathic Morse message over a distance of 1,200 miles (2,000 kilometres) between New York and Florida.

But despite these discoveries and the outstanding individual results that some experiments have produced, not all researchers are so successful when they attempt to duplicate telepathy tests. 'Mental radio' remains an elusive phenomenon, although it is one that has occurred often enough – spontaneously and in the laboratory.

THE POWER TO OVERCOME THE FORCE OF GRAVITY IS SAID SOMETIMES TO OCCUR SPONTANEOUSLY, AMAZING LEVITATOR AND ONLOOKERS ALIKE. HOW REAL IS THE PHENOMENON?

DEFYING THE LAW OF GRAVITY

Three notable members of London society witnessed, on 16 December 1868, an incident so extraordinary that it is still a focus of controversy. Viscount Adare, the Master of Lindsay and Captain Wynne saw the famous medium Daniel Home rise into the air and float out of one window in a large house in fashionable London and then float in at another – over 80 feet (24 metres) from the ground, it is claimed. D.D. Home became known primarily for his levitations, of himself and of objects – on one occasion, a grand piano – but he was not alone in having this apparently 'impossible' ability to defy the law of gravity.

St Joseph of Copertino (1603-1663) flew into the air every time he was emotionally aroused. Being of an excitable nature, he often made levitations, and they were well witnessed. A simple peasant – some say he was actually feeble-minded – this boy, from Apulia in Italy, spent his youth trying to achieve religious ecstasy by such means as self-flagellation, starvation and wearing hair-shirts. He became a Franciscan at the age of 22, and then his religious fervour 'took off', quite literally.

D.D. Home, above, ascribed his levitations to the work of spirits, and is seen, above right, floating into the air with no visible means of support.

SAINTLY GIDDINESS

Joseph soon became something of an embarrassment to his superiors. During Mass one Sunday, he rose into the air and flew onto the altar in the midst of the candles, becoming badly burned as a result.

For 35 years, Joseph was excluded from all public services because of his disconcerting habits, but still tales of his levitations spread. While walking with a Benedictine monk in the monastery gardens, for instance, he suddenly flew up into an olive tree. Unfortunately he was unable to fly back down, so his fellow-monks had to fetch a ladder.

A surgeon, at least two cardinals and one Pope (Urban VIII), among many others, witnessed Joseph's extraordinary spells of weightlessness – which he called 'my giddinesses' – and the Church concluded the levitations must be the work of God.

Another levitator was St Teresa of Avila, who died in 1582. This remarkable mystic experienced the same feelings as many people do during common 'flying dreams'.

'It seemed to me, when I tried to make some resistance, as if a great force beneath my

St Joseph of Copertino, depicted below, owed his canonisation to an ability to levitate.

feet lifted me up ... I confess that it threw me into great fear, very great indeed at first; for in seeing one's body thus lifted up from the earth, though the spirit draws it upwards after itself (and that with great sweetness, if unresisted), the senses are not lost; at least I was so much myself as able to see that I was being lifted up. After the rapture was over, I have to say my body seemed frequently to be buoyant, as if all weight had departed from it, so much so that now and then I scarce knew my feet touched the ground', she said.

Indeed, so insistent were St Teresa's levitations that she begged the sisters to hold her down when she felt an 'attack' coming on, but often there was no time for such measures – she simply rose off the floor until the weightlessness passed.

Most levitators are believers in one particular system, be it Christianity, Hindu mysticism, ancient Egyptian mysteries or Spiritualism; and it was to this last category that D.D. Home belonged.

Born in Scotland and brought up in America, Home was a puny, artistic child. At the age of 13, he had a vision of a friend, Edwin, and announced to his aunt's family that this must mean that Edwin had been dead for three days. Amazingly, it was proved to be true. Home's career as a medium had begun; but it was not until he was 19 that he would actually defy the law of gravity.

Colin Evans, top, seems to drift aloft at the Conway Hall, London, in the 1930s.

St Teresa of Avila, above, was also subject to 'attacks of levitation.

Away from all artificial aids, the couple, left, appears to defeat the force of gravity on a South African beach in 1962.

Ward Cheney, a prosperous silk-manufacturer, held a seance at his home in Connecticut in August 1852, and D.D. Home was there to provide the usual 'spiritualist' manifestations – table-turning, rappings, floating trumpets and mysterious lights.

Home was quite capable of keeping the guests entertained in this fashion; but something happened, completely unannounced, that made his name overnight. He suddenly floated up into the air until his head was touching the ceiling.

UP TO THE CEILING

Among the guests was a sceptical reporter, F.L. Burr, editor of the *Hartford Times*. He wrote of this bizarre and unexpected incident:

'Suddenly, without any expectation on the part of the company, Home was taken up into the air. I had hold of his hand at the time and I felt his feet – they were lifted a foot (30 centimetres) from the floor. He palpitated from head to foot with the contending emotions of joy and fear which choked his utterances. Again and again he was taken from the floor, and the third time he was carried to the ceiling of the apartment, with which his hands and feet came into gentle contact.'

Home's career advanced rapidly and he was lionised in seance parlour and royal court alike. Indeed, wherever he went there were bizarre phenomena – winds howled in still rooms, apports of fresh flowers fell from the ceiling, doors opened and shut, fireballs zigzagged around the room – and Home levitated.

The famous occasion, when he floated out of one window and in through another, is still the subject of heated debate, particularly since the incident was documented by respectable witnesses. One of

them, the Master of Lindsay (later the Earl of Crawford) wrote:

'I was sitting with Mr Home and Lord Adare and a cousin of his [Captain Wynne]. During the sitting, Mr Home went into a trance and in that state was carried out of the window in the room next to where we were, and was brought in at our window. The distance between the windows was about seven feet six inches [2.3 metres], and there was not the slightest foothold between them, nor was there more than a 12-inch [30 centimetres] projection to each window, which served as a ledge to put flowers on. We heard the window in the next room lift up, and almost immediately after we saw Home floating in the air outside our window. The moon was shining full into the room; my back was to the light, and I saw the shadow on the wall of the windowsill, and Home's feet about six inches [15 centimetres] above it. He remained in this position for a few seconds, then raised the window and glided into the room feet foremost and sat down.'

SUBTLE SCEPTICISM

Sceptics such as Frank Podmore or, more recently, John Sladek, have tried to disprove this levitation, although neither of them was among the witnesses. Sladek attempted to discredit the three who were present by comparing the details of their stories – such as how high the balconies were from the street or, indeed, whether there were actually any balconies at all.

Podmore, on the other hand, was more subtle in his scepticism. He mentions the fact that a few days before the levitation, and in front of the same witnesses, Home had opened the window and stood on the ledge outside. He had pointedly drawn their attention to himself standing on the narrow ledge some considerable distance from the ground. As Podmore remarked drily: 'The medium had thus,

In a classic stage levitation, top, *the girl, Marva Ganzel, is first hypnotised into a cataleptic trance while balanced on two swords. When one is taken away, she somehow remains suspended in mid-air.*
Frank Podmore, above, *suggested that D.D. Home's most famous levitation was merely an hallucination.*

Accounts of levitation and other manifestations of the seance room obviously did not impress Punch *which, in 1863, published the lampoon,* right, *showing that some surprises, at least, could be administered by all too explicable means.*

as it were, furnished a rough sketch of the picture which he aimed at producing.'

On another occasion, Home suddenly announced 'I'm rising, I'm rising', before proceeding to levitate in front of several witnesses. Again, Podmore implied that Home's levitations were nothing more than hallucinations produced by his hypnotic suggestion, rather in the same manner that the Indian rope trick is said to be a mass hallucination, the secret being in the magician's patter.

But even in the face of extreme hostility, Home remained a successful levitator for over 40 years. Among his witnesses were Emperor Napoleon III, John Ruskin and many hundreds more, not all of whom were as inconsistent in their testimonies as Adare, Wynne and Lindsay. Moreover, during that long span of time and mostly in broad daylight, Home was never proven to be a fraud. And despite Podmore's accusations, Home never went out of his way to build up an atmosphere heavy with suggestibility. In fact, he was one of the few mediums actively to eschew 'atmosphere'. He preferred a normal or bright light to darkness and encouraged sitters to chat in a relaxed fashion rather than 'hold hands and concentrate'.

Although, in his mature years, Home could levitate at will, he apparently also levitated without being aware of it. On one occasion, for example, when his host drew his attention to the fact that he was hovering above the cushions of his armchair, Home seemed most surprised.

Stage illusionists frequently pride themselves on their *pièce de résistance* – putting their assistant into a 'trance', balancing her on the points of two swords, and then removing the swords so that she hangs in the air without apparent support. Sometimes she is 'hypnotised' and seen to rise further into the air, again without visible means of support. One of two things must be happening: either she does not rise into the air at all (that is, we all suffer some sort of mass hallucination), or she rises

aided by machinery that is hidden and therefore invisible to us.

Home was also able to make tables levitate, complete with any objects that happened to be on them; and when he raised a grand piano into the air, he also levitated the astounded Countess Orsini, who was playing it at the time. But his amazing talents did not stop there. Home could also elongate his physical form, and was able to hold hot coals without flinching.

Of course, Home and other spiritualists would also attribute their feats of apportation or levitation to 'machinery invisible to us' – but in their case, the machinery would be the agency of spirits. Indeed, to the end of his life, Home maintained that he could only fly because he was lifted up by the spirits, who thus demonstrated their existence. He described a typical levitation as follows:

'I feel no hands supporting me and, since the first time, I have never felt fear; though, should I have fallen from the ceiling of some rooms in which I have been raised, I could not have escaped serious injury. I am generally lifted up perpendicular!'

And yet we do not refer in a spiritualistic way to the 'unseen power' that keeps us on the floor. Every schoolboy knows about Newton and his discovery of the law of gravity. But psychical research points to the relative ease with which certain sensitives can turn this law on its head.

MYSTICAL TRAINING

In her book *Mystère et Magique en Tibet* (1931), Madame Alexandra David-Neel, the French explorer who spent 14 years in and around Tibet, told how she came upon a naked man, weighed down with heavy chains. The man's companion explained to her that his mystical training had made his body so light that, unless he wore iron chains, he would float away.

It seems that gravity does not necessarily always have the hold on us we have been taught it has. Sir William Crookes, the renowned scientist and psychical researcher, had this to say about D.D. Home's levitations:

'The phenomena I am prepared to attest are so extraordinary, and so directly oppose the most firmly-rooted articles of scientific belief – amongst others, the ubiquity and invariable action of the force of gravitation – that, even now, on recalling the details of what I have witnessed, there is an antagonism in my mind between reason, which pronounces it to be scientifically impossible, and the consciousness that my senses, both of touch and sight, are not lying witnesses.'

In some special cases – such as saints or particularly gifted mediums – levitation may well exist. But there is a growing body of thought that puts forward the idea that anyone can do it, providing he or she has been through the right sort of training. Students of transcendental meditation even claim to do it all the time.

▎▎I FEEL NO HANDS SUPPORTING ME AND, SINCE THE FIRST TIME, I HAVE NEVER FELT FEAR; THOUGH, SHOULD I HAVE FALLEN FROM THE CEILING OF SOME ROOMS IN WHICH I HAVE BEEN RAISED, I COULD NOT HAVE ESCAPED SERIOUS INJURY. I AM GENERALLY LIFTED UP PERPENDICULAR! **▎▎**

D.D. HOME

THE POWER BEHIND THE HUNCH

COULD THE 'HUNCHES' ON WHICH MANY EXECUTIVES SEEM TO RELY BE EXTRA-SENSORY IN THEIR ORIGIN?

After a two-year development programme costing $2 million, the Electric Hydracon Company in Altoona, Pennsylvania, USA, discovered a serious flaw in its new extruded metal installation, which moulds metal by pushing it through dies. Only when the work was completed did the company realise that, if the machinery were run continuously, the regular dies and tooling used would last only a week.

'Financial disaster would be our reward,' said Richard Haupt, who was then executive vice-president. He consulted five major companies to see what could be done and they all gave the same advice. If Electric Hydracon wanted its new plant to last longer, it had to use harder materials for the container, dies and tooling. But Haupt had a nagging doubt: somehow he was sure that it would be better to use softer materials.

'Our president directed me to abide by the decision of the major steel mills,' Haupt recalled.

At the New York Stock Exchange, above, in the Wall Street district, right, many of the men who successfully play the Market admit that they are often guided by precognition and other forms of extra-sensory perception.

'Nevertheless, I followed my own intuition and spent two-and-a-half times more money for the softer material. The result was an outstanding success with the softer tooling. It lasts six times as long as harder steels. The entire industry has now followed this procedure.'

Richard Haupt, like many other top executives, recognises that there are times when an element of extra-sensory perception emerges in his decision-making, urging him to follow a course of action that often flies in the face of logic or expert advice. This talent, dubbed 'executive ESP', has been the subject of several studies.

PSYCHIC ACUMEN

Most businessmen would deny that they were psychic, and it is admittedly difficult to know where subconscious assessment for normal sensory clues ends, and extra-sensory perception begins. Executives who recognise that there is a difference between the two use many different words to describe it: sixth sense, business acumen, gut feeling, hunch or intuition.

Psychical researcher Dr Douglas Dean says that executive ESP is an essential ingredient in business life where decisions have to be made about future events, often without enough information to justify them. 'Businessmen use it every week, every month, every year, continually. And the best ones go on doing it very happily without worrying about it. They pile up tremendous profits year after year because they really are stupendous at this ability.'

This statement is based on the research he carried out with the PSI Communications Project at Newark College of Engineering, New Jersey. An English electrochemist with a keen interest in the paranormal, Dean worked on the project with a professor of industrial engineering who was originally sceptical – Dr John Mihalasky.

Among those who gave financial support to the project was the late Chester Carlson, inventor of the Xerox photocopying technique, who – through personal experience – had no doubts at all about the existence of ESP and other psychic phenomena, and often used his special abilities to advantage.

During the course of the PSI Communications Project, the researchers interviewed many top executives and looked at the lives of others. William C. Durant, the founder of General Motors, was typical. One of his colleagues, Alfred P. Sloan, a former president of the giant automobile company, said Durant, 'would proceed on a course of action guided solely, as far as I could tell, by some intuitive flash of brilliance. He never felt obliged to make an engineering hunt for the facts.'

Choosing the right sites for his hotels was the responsibility of Charles Kemmons Wilson, founder and chairman of Holiday Inns Inc. He described the task as like 'going on an Easter egg hunt and sometimes you find the golden egg'. There were times when he would insist on weeks of study by his company before he would make a decision on a site. But there were other times when he would give an emphatic 'no' for no other reason than 'I don't like the smell of it'.

Another hotel man who believed in following his hunches was Conrad Hilton. In the 1940s, Hilton advised Duncan Harris, president of a large real

Dr Douglas Dean, above left, together with Dr John Mihalasky, carried out extensive research into the role of ESP in business life. Among the many top executives whose lives and achievements he examined were Conrad Hilton, top left, international hotel magnate; William C. Durant, top right, founder of General Motors; Charles Kemmons Wilson, above, chairman of Holiday Inns; and Charles Chester Carlson, below, inventor of the Xerox photocopying technique.

estate firm, to buy Waldorf-Astoria bonds. Hilton himself had snapped up a considerable number at 4½ cents, much to the surprise of other businessmen. The Depression had made the bonds tumble in price and wartime was adding to the difficulties of maintaining hotels.

Harris was sceptical about his friend's advice and he invited Hilton to listen in on an extension when he telephoned his broker about the bonds. 'Some wild man from the West has forced them up to 8 cents,' said the broker with amusement. 'We're unloading by the bushel. This is the first time in years that anyone holding hotel paper has believed in Santa Claus.'

The cynicism did not dismay Hilton, who remarked later: 'Harris bought, and so, sweating and swearing, did a small faithful group who backed Connie's hunches. Later, hotel securities boomed and the wild man who bought at 4½ cents was considered an astute fellow when he sold at 85 cents. Santa Claus had planted $22,500 and reaped almost $500,000. I've been accused more than once of playing hunches... I further believe most people have them, whether they follow them or not.'

Another of Hilton's hunches paid off when, during the war, he made a bid for the Stevens Corporation. He had wanted the Stevens Hotel, Chicago, but it had been taken over by the Air Force. He decided, when the Stevens Corporation came on the market, that its assets might prove profitable and, in time, if ever the government released the Chicago hotel, it would be his. But the Corporation's trustees called for sealed bids. The business empire would go to the highest bidder. In such a situation, interested parties run the risk of losing a bid by a narrow margin, or unnecessarily outbidding their rivals by many thousands.

There are other ways, too, it seems – apart from relying on hunches – of tapping into financial success. Alison Harper, above, operates as an astrologer, and uses her predictions to help British businessmen make the right commercial decisions. One office systems company even has her on a retainer, contacting her regularly for advice.

The 1906 San Francisco earthquake destroyed miles of track belonging to the Union Pacific railway, right, and the company's stock fell drastically as a result. But one stockholder, Jesse Livermore, saved himself over a quarter of a million dollars: only a few days before, he had obeyed an impulse to 'sell short on Union Pacific'.

'No businessman likes sealed bids,' Hilton remarked. 'My first bid, hastily made, was $165,000. Then somehow it didn't feel right to me. Another figure kept coming, $180,000. It satisfied me. It seemed fair. It felt right. I changed my bid to the larger figure on that hunch. When the sealed bids were opened , the closest to mine was $179,800. So I got the Stevens Corporation by a narrow margin of $200. Eventually the assets returned me $2 million.'

INTUITIVE BIDDING

A similar situation arose in 1969 when the Alaskan oil lands were sold off. The international oil companies also had to make sealed bids, and one particular area of six square miles (16 square kilometres) was of interest to many of them, including the Amarada-Hess-Getty Oil Combine. It had already made a bid but, suddenly, on the weekend before the land was awarded, Leon Hess decided to increase the amount he was prepared to pay to $72.3 million. If he had not done so, he would have lost. When the bids were announced, his combine's offer was just $200,000 above its nearest competitor. Why did Leon Hess decide to boost his offer? 'I suddenly had a hunch,' he explained.

Playing the Stock Market successfully may also depend at times on a willingness to follow hunches. Jesse Livermore, a Wall Street multi-millionaire with intuitive talents was so confident of his ESP powers that he even interrupted a holiday in order to obey a hunch to 'sell short on Union Pacific'. It was a strange decision to make because the railway's stock looked as solid as a rock, but he obeyed the impulse. A few days later, the San Francisco earthquake wrecked miles of the railway company's track and its stock fell drastically. The hunch netted Livermore over a quarter of a million dollars.

So what is a hunch? The top executives who rely on it do not seen to know. Benjamin Fairless, former Chairman of the Board of US Steel, has said: 'You don't know how you do it; you just do it.'

It would seem that executive ESP is often a deciding factor in an individual's business career, enabling those who possess the gift to rise to the top and help their companies to prosper. But would it be possible to spot such people in advance? Surprisingly, the answer which the PSI Communications Project came up with is 'Yes'. Dean and Mihalasky, as well as interviewing top businessmen and actually testing them for ESP, also examined their outlook in a search for clues that would differentiate between those who had produced high scores in the tests and those who, as it turned out, scored below average.

❚❚ MY FIRST BID, HASTILY MADE, WAS $165,000. THEN SOMEHOW IT DIDN'T FEEL RIGHT TO ME. ANOTHER FIGURE KEPT COMING, $180,000. IT SATISFIED ME... IT FELT RIGHT... SO I GOT THE STEVENS CORPORATION BY A NARROW MARGIN OF $200. EVENTUALLY THE ASSETS RETURNED ME $2 MILLION. **❚❚**

CONRAD HILTON

They were greatly influenced by the work of a leading American psychical researcher, Dr Gertrude Schmeidler, professor of psychology at the City College of New York. Dr Schmeidler had been investigating precognition for some considerable time and had compared the results of the participants in her experiments with their responses to a specially devised, so-called Time Metaphor Test. Individuals were asked if they thought of time as a dashing waterfall, a motionless sea, or in the form of an old man.

Those whose images of time were fast-moving were classed as 'dynamics', whereas those who regarded it as a motionless sea were said to be 'naturalistics'. For the few for whom time conjured up an image of an old man, the term 'humanistic' was used – they were the neutrals. When Dr Schmeidler analysed her results she discovered that the dynamics scored high in precognition tests, where they knew they would subsequently be told the outcome.

Time and again in these tests, the two Newark researchers found dynamics out-scoring naturalistics (whom they called oceanics) in the ESP tests,

which usually involved attempting to guess a number they set participants, that a computer would generate randomly.

DYNAMIC SCORES

On one occasion, 40 top-flight executives were subjected to a test. Once again, the dynamics, as a group, outscored their oceanic colleagues. This time, Mihalasky also compared the results with the financial success of each individual's company. As he commented:

'Some of the presidents were company owners. I asked if they were also the chief decision makers. If the answer was no, I discarded them. Others were chief decision makers but didn't have the title of president, and I threw them out too.' In this way he reduced the number to a dozen, all of whom were presidents who had held office for at least five years.

'Of these,' Mihalasky reports, 'every man who improved his company's profits by 100 per cent or more scored above the ten mark (average) on the precognition test.' He then combined the statistics with those attained at a similar survey of top executives, giving him 25 chief executives of small, medium and large companies. Twelve of these ran companies which had performed outstandingly, at least doubling profits in five years. When he checked their scores in the ESP test, he found that 11 of the 12 scored above average, and the twelfth man scored exactly at chance. Not one of them showed a negative ESP score.

An examination of the other 13 chief executives, who had not doubled their profits in five years, showed that five who had scored above chance had improved profits by between 51 and 100 per cent. One man scored at chance level, and of the seven who scored below chance only two had improved profits by more than 50 per cent.

Though not a large enough study to claim proof of the theory, these results do suggest very strongly that there is a correlation between profit-making and ESP abilities.

MUSIC FROM BEYON THE GRAVE

A NUMBER OF SENSITIVES CLAIM TO RECEIVE
WORKS FROM LONG-DEAD COMPOSERS. BUT ARE
THESE WORKS TRULY FROM THE SPIRIT WORLD,
OR DO THEY COME FROM THE
SUBCONSCIOUS MIND?

Beethoven is even now working on a new symphony. This extraordinary concept – that musicians and other creative beings can produce works of art years, even centuries, after their death – is as natural as breathing to many spiritualists and psychics.

The best known of those mediums who claim to be amanuenses for long-dead composers is London housewife Rosemary Brown, who in the past has acted almost as an agent for Liszt, Beethoven, Brahms, Debussy, Chopin, Schubert and, more recently, Stravinsky. She is an unassuming lady with only a rudimentary musical background, and she is the first to acknowledge that the works 'dictated' to her are beyond her everyday musical capacity. Rosemary Brown sees herself merely as the humble scribe and friend of the late composers – the ultimate polish must come from the professionals in performance.

The idea of survival beyond death is not, however, strange to this suburban housewife. As a young

Rosemary Brown, above left, 'wrote' Mazurka in D flat, above. She claims to have been inspired by the spirit of Chopin, above right, while being filmed by an American television company in October 1980.

Beethoven, shown left, contacted Rosemary Brown in 1964, when he told her he was no longer deaf and again enjoyed listening to music.

Rosemary Brown sought an interview with American composer and conductor Leonard Bernstein, below right, on the advice of her 'spirits'. He is said to have been most impressed with the music Rosemary showed him.

her conscious capacity or even her conscious knowledge. During these sessions, Rosemary Brown would chat so naturally with her unseen guests that it is difficult to be embarrassed, despite the bizarre circumstances. Pen poised over the music sheets, she would listen. 'I see...', she would say to Franz Liszt, 'these two bars go here... no, I see, I'm sorry. No, you're getting too fast for me. If you could just repeat...' With pauses for checking and some conversation with the composer, she would write down the work far faster than most musicians could possibly compose.

But sometimes communications were interrupted, as she gently chided Liszt for becoming so excited that he spoke volubly in German or French. Chopin occasionally forgot himself and spoke to her in his native Polish – which she would write down phonetically and have translated by a Polish friend.

RECOGNISABLE STYLES

So are these posthumous works recognisably those of Liszt, Chopin, Beethoven, Brahms? Concert pianist Hephzibah Menuhin put it this way: 'I look at

girl, she had visions of an elderly man who told her repeatedly that he and other great composers would befriend her and teach her their wonderful music. It was only many years later, when she was a widow, concerned mainly with the struggle of bringing up two children alone and on very limited means, that she saw a picture of Franz Liszt (1811-1886) and recognised him immediately as her ghostly friend.

In 1964, she was contacted by other great composers, among them Beethoven and Chopin, and her life work – taking down their 'unfinished symphonies' – then began in earnest.

The pieces transmitted to her are no mere outlines but full compositions, mainly for the piano but some for full orchestras. Rosemary Brown says the music was already composed when it was communicated to her: the musicians simply dictated it as fast as she could write it down.

Indeed, observers of the process have been amazed at the speed with which Rosemary Brown wrote the music – and the standard is far beyond

Franz Liszt, right, first appeared to Rosemary Brown when she was a young girl. He told her that, when she grew up, he and other composers would contact her and teach her their music.

these manuscripts with immense respect. Each piece is distinctly in the composer's style.' Leonard Bernstein and his wife entertained Rosemary Brown in their London hotel suite and were very impressed both by her sincerity and by the music, purportedly from the long-dead composers, she took to them. British composer Richard Rodney Bennett said: 'A lot of people can improvise, but you couldn't fake music like this without years of training. I couldn't have faked some of the Beethoven myself'.

Since that memorable breakthrough in 1964, Rosemary Brown claims also to have been contacted by dead artists, poets, playwrights, philosophers and scientists. Vincent van Gogh (1853-1890) has communicated current works through her – at first in charcoal ('because that's all I had') and then in oils. But Debussy has chosen to paint through Rosemary Brown, rather than compose, because his artistic interests have changed since he has 'passed over'.

Apparently, the philosopher Bertrand Russell has also had to reconsider his atheism and disbelief in a life after death for, as Rosemary Brown points out, he is very much 'alive' these days and wants to pass on the message of hope in eternal life. Albert Einstein has also communicated, patiently explaining any difficult jargon or concepts, and reinforcing the belief in further planes of existence.

Sceptics are often quick to spot that the music alleged to come from the minds of the great composers is less than their best, and reminiscent of their earliest, rather than their mature, works. This, says Rosemary Brown, is not the point. Her first introduction to Franz Liszt was 'more than a musical break-through'. Indeed, the late Sir Donald Tovey is said to have explained the motivation behind such communications in a posthumous statement:

'In communicating through music and conversation, an organized group of musicians, who have departed from your world, are attempting to establish a precept for humanity, i.e., that physical death is a transition from one state of consciousness to another wherein one retains one's individuality... We are not transmitting music to Rosemary Brown simply for the sake of offering possible pleasure in listening thereto; it is the implications relevant to

Rosemary Brown's contacts are not confined to the field of music. Vincent Van Gogh inspired the drawing, right, in 1975; and Debussy, below, now more interested in visual art, also paints 'through' her. She was contacted by Albert Einstein, bottom, in 1967, and by Bertrand Russell, below left, in 1973.

the phenomenon which we hope will stimulate sensible and sensitive interest and stir many who are intelligent and impartial to consider and explore the unknown of man's mind and psyche. When man has plumbed the mysterious depths of his veiled consciousness, he will then be able to soar to correspondingly greater heights.'

Rosemary Brown has many friends and admirers outside the spiritualist circle, notably among distinguished musicians, writers and broadcasters. Whatever the source of her mysterious music, this modest and religious lady inspires respect and affection, so obvious is her sincerity.

She is, however, not unique in her musical communications. The British concert pianist, John Lill, also claims an other-worldly inspiration for his playing. This winner of the prestigious Tchaikovsky Piano Competition had a tough beginning, playing the piano in pubs in London's East End. As he says 'I don't go around like a crazed fellow with my head in the air... I'm neither a nutter nor some quaint loony falling around in a state of trance'. But, as he has added thoughtfully, 'because something is rare it doesn't mean that it doesn't exist'.

That 'something' began for him when he was practising in the Moscow Conservatoire for the Tchaikovsky Piano Competition. He became aware of a figure watching him – someone wearing unusual clothes. He believes he was being observed by Beethoven, who later held many conversations with him. However, John Lill does not consider himself a special case. This sort of direct inspiration, he says, is available to everyone who achieves a certain frame of mind:

'It is very difficult to conceive inspiration unless it is something you receive. I don't see it as something from within a person. When I go on stage, I close my mind to what I have learnt and open it fully in the expectation that inspiration will be received.'

Concert pianist John Lill, right, is convinced that he, too, has had spiritual help in his career. He believes that Beethoven watched him practising for the Tchaikovsky Piano Competition in Moscow, and has since held several conversations with him. Beethoven has even dedicated a piece of his own music to him – the Sonata in E Minor, communicated to Rosemary Brown in 1972.

Clifford Enticknap, below, wrote an oratorio entitled Beyond the Veil *'under the inspiration' of G.F. Handel, shown bottom.*

❝ WE ARE NOT TRANSMITTING MUSIC TO ROSEMARY BROWN SIMPLY FOR THE SAKE OF OFFERING POSSIBLE PLEASURE... IT IS THE IMPLICATIONS RELEVANT TO THIS PHENOMENON WHICH WE HOPE WILL STIMULATE SENSIBLE AND SENSITIVE INTEREST AND STIR MANY WHO ARE INTELLIGENT AND AND IMPARTIAL TO CONSIDER AND EXPLORE THE UNKNOWN OF MAN'S MIND AND PSYCHE. **❞**

SIR DONALD TOVEY,
POSTHUMOUSLY

But sometimes it is difficult to achieve this state of mind 'if it is a particularly muggy day, or the acoustics are dry. Even the attitude of the audience makes a difference. A quiet mind is essential,' according to Lill.

The composer of, among other magnificent works, the Messiah, also wrote grand oratorios through his medium Clifford Enticknap, an Englishman obsessed with Handel. The great composer taught him music in another incarnation, says Enticknap, and their relationship as master and pupil dates back to the time of Atlantis where Handel was a great teacher known as Joseph Arkos. Yet, before that, the soul we know as Handel lived on Jupiter, the planet of music, together with all the souls we know as the great musicians (and some we may never know for they will not be incarnated on Earth), Enticknap has revealed.

BEYOND THE VEIL

In his personality as 'the master Handel', the musician communicated to Enticknap a four-and-a-half-hour long oratorio entitled *Beyond the Veil*. A 73-minute excerpt of this has been recorded by the London Symphony Orchestra and the Handelian Foundation Choir, available on tape through the Handelian Foundation as 'proof' of Handel's survival beyond death.

In BBC-TV's programme *Spirits from the Past*, shown on 12 August 1980, snatches from the oratorio were played over scenes of Mr Enticknap playing the organ in Handel's favourite English church. Television critics found little fault with the music – which did indeed sound to the untutored ear to be very similar to Handel's more familiar works – but the words provoked widespread ridicule. Once critic compared them with the unfortunate poetry of William McGonagall (1805-1902) whose poetic sincerity was matched only by his total lack of talent and sheer genius in juxtaposing the risible with the

pathetic. (Another critic went so far as to exclaim: 'Fame at last for McGonagall – he's teamed up with Handel beyond the veil!')

However, mediums warn against judging spirit communications in a state of flippant scepticism. As John Lill says of the difficulties that the spirits sometimes have in 'getting through': 'It's all to do with cleaning a window, and some windows are cleaner than others'.

POOL OF KNOWLEDGE

If, as many serious researchers into the paranormal have believed, the music does not in fact come from the minds of deceased musicians, then where does it come from? It is certainly not from the conscious mind of Rosemary Brown, who obviously struggled to keep up with the dictation.

Some psychics believe that our deeper inspirations are culled from the 'Akashic records' or 'Book of Life', wherein lies all knowledge. In certain states of mind, experienced by some especially sensitive people, this hidden knowledge becomes available to the human consciousness. Rosemary Brown could well be one of these remarkably receptive people; and the music she believes comes from Chopin or Beethoven may come instead from this 'pool' of musical knowledge.

The late Rosemary Rosalind Heywood, researcher into the paranormal, and author of *The Sixth Sense*, has another suggestion. Rosemary Brown is, she guesses, 'the type of sensitive whom frustration, often artistic, drives to the automatic production of material beyond their conscious capacity'.

To those who believe in the omniscience of the human subconscious, the compositions given to the world by Rosemary Brown and others like her raise more questions than they answer. But it is all so beautifully simply to the mediums: there is no death and genius is eternal.

THOUGHT-OGRAPHY:
FANTASY OR REALITY?

ARE THE IMAGES PRODUCED BY TED SERIOS PROOF THAT THOUGHTS CAN BE PROJECTED ON TO FILM?

One of the few colour 'thoughtographs' produced by Serios is shown, right. He was aiming at a target picture of the Hilton hotel at Denver, but obtained this image of the Chicago Hilton instead.

The picture below was produced by Serios for researcher Dr Jule Eisenbud. It was immediately identified by one of the observers at the session as the Chicago Water Tower, below right. Only later was it recognised as part of the Kremlin, an image of which Eisenbud had hidden in an envelope handed to Serios.

Ted Serios sat down in the hotel room and pointed a Polaroid camera at his face. The flashbulb fired. Dr Jule Eisenbud immediately took the camera from him and pulled the print from the back. Instead of Serios' face, however, the unmistakable image of a building appeared.

For Serios – a chain-smoking, alcoholic Chicago bell-hop – it was just another of his strange psychic images known as 'thoughtographs'. But for Dr Eisenbud, an associate professor of psychiatry at the University of Colorado Medical School, it was such an impressive demonstration of paranormal power that he went on to study Serios for several years and also wrote a book about him.

When Dr Eisenbud flew to Chicago for the first experimental session with the hard-drinking psychic

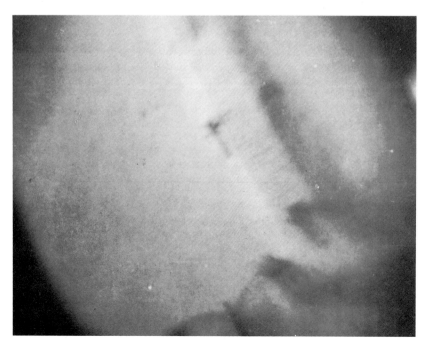

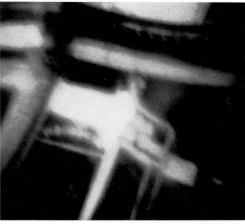

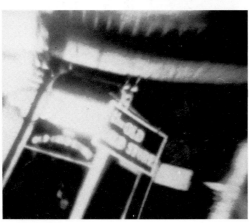

black, even though the room lighting and other factors remained constant. Occasionally, the image that emerged from the Polaroid covered the whole area of the print, while at other times it obliterated only a portion of Serios or identifiable items in the room where the experiment is being conducted. The Eiffel Tower, Big Ben, the White House and orbiting satellites all feature in his album of thoughtographs.

In his early days, Serios just looked at the camera to produce his startling pictures, but later he introduced a 'gismo', which he held in front of the lens while concentrating. Sometimes he used a small plastic cylinder, one end of which was covered with plain cellophane, the other with cellophane over a piece of blackened film; on other occasions, he simply rolled up a piece of paper.

SECRETS OF THE 'GISMO'

The purpose of the 'gismo', Serios said, was to keep his fingers from obscuring the lens. His critics, however, have seen it as having a far more sinister purpose. It could very easily have concealed a 'gimmick', containing microfilm or a transparency, they argued; and, for them, its use became as suspicious as a conjuror's hat.

Two reporters, Charles Reynolds and David Eisendrath, constructed a small device that could be hidden in a 'gismo' and that produced similar-looking results to those of Serios. Their account, published in *Popular Photography* in October 1967, gave sceptics all the 'evidence' they needed.

The images above are two of 11 views of a shop front in Central City, Colorado, produced by Ted Serios, left. At the time, the building was used as a tourist shop called the 'Old Wells Fargo Express Office'. Several years previously, however, it had been called 'The Old Gold Store', of which no photographs were known to exist.

❝ INVESTIGATORS WHO WORKED WITH SERIOS SUPPLIED THEIR OWN FILM AND CAMERAS; SOMETIMES THEY EVEN TOOK THE PICTURES THEMSELVES, WITH THE CAMERA POINTING AT THE CHICAGO PSYCHIC – THE RESULTS WERE FREQUENTLY VERY STRANGE INDEED. ❞

Eisenbud and other researchers, on the other hand, were satisfied that the 'gismo' contained no hidden equipment, and that Serios did not slip anything inside it just before an exposure was made. They were all aware of the hidden microfilm hypothesis, and evolved an experimental protocol to overcome it. Serios was usually given the 'gismo' when he felt he could produce a paranormal print. It was then taken from him immediately and examined. It was probably in his hands for no longer than 15 seconds at a time, and throughout that period was under close scrutiny.

At the sessions, Serios usually wore short-sleeved shirts or stripped to the waist, making it impossible for him to conceal anything close to his hands. Besides, researchers have said, they were frequently close enough to the action when Serios told them to fire the camera that they could actually

photographer in April 1964, he was almost certain that he was about to witness 'some kind of shoddy hoax'. Because of his interest in the paranormal, Eisenbud was aware that there had been many so-called psychic photographers over the years who had been caught cheating, usually by tampering with their film. But the appearance of the Polaroid camera had changed that, making it easier to control the production of such 'thoughtographic' prints, as well as giving results in seconds.

Investigators who worked with Serios supplied their own film and cameras; and sometimes even took the pictures themselves, with the camera pointing at the Chicago psychic. The results that emerged were frequently very strange indeed. Not all the photographs carried images, though; some were unusually white, while others were totally

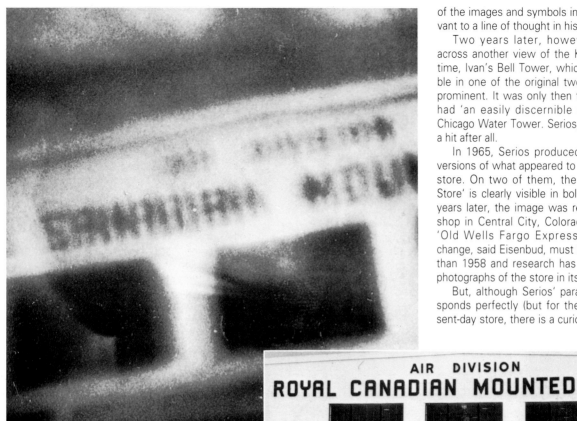

of the images and symbols in the picture were relevant to a line of thought in his mind at the time.

Two years later, however, Eisenbud came across another view of the Kremlin buildings. This time, Ivan's Bell Tower, which was only partly visible in one of the original two target pictures, was prominent. It was only then that he realised that it had 'an easily discernible resemblance' to the Chicago Water Tower. Serios, it seems, had scored a hit after all.

In 1965, Serios produced 11 slightly different versions of what appeared to be the glass front of a store. On two of them, the name 'The Old Gold Store' is clearly visible in bold block lettering. Two years later, the image was recognised as a tourist shop in Central City, Colorado, which is now the 'Old Wells Fargo Express Office'. The name change, said Eisenbud, must have occurred no later than 1958 and research has failed to unearth any photographs of the store in its earlier days.

But, although Serios' paranormal picture corresponds perfectly (but for the name) with the present-day store, there is a curious substitution in one

see through the 'gismo' and check that it contained no hidden devices.

On numerous occasions, images even appeared when someone else was holding the 'gismo' and the camera, and so was able to examine both freely. Two eminent American psychical researchers, Dr J.G. Pratt and Dr Ian Stevenson, who conducted numerous tests with Serios, have stated: 'We have ourselves observed Ted in approximately 800 trials and we have never seen him act in a suspicious way in the handling of the gismo before or after a trial'. Quite apart from the fact that Serios was never caught with any hidden transparencies or microfilm, Dr Eisenbud also argued that the very nature of the images that Serios produced rules out the 'gimmick' theory.

TARGET PICTURES

On some occasions, Serios invited investigators to bring with them target pictures concealed in envelopes, which he tried to reproduce paranormally on Polaroid film. On the first occasion that Eisenbud saw Serios produce a paranormal picture, in a Chicago hotel room, the psychiatrist had taken with him two views of the Kremlin buildings, each hidden in a cardboard-backed envelope.

One of the images that Serios produced at that session was of a tall, thin building, which a witness immediately identified as the Chicago Water Tower – a landmark that would have been familiar to Serios. Though this seemed to be totally off target, Eisenbud was very impressed, partly because some

The blurred lettering on the 'thoughtograph', top, enabled researchers to identify the building as a hanger belonging to the Air Division of the Royal Canadian Mounted Police, above. The picture bears the stamp of Ted Serios in the misspelling 'CAINADAIN'.

The nude, far right, is another example of what is claimed to have been achieved by the power of thought and a single sheet of photographic paper.

picture of the letter 'W' for 'O' so that it reads 'The Wld Gold Store'. And the 'W' is exactly where it would be if 'Wells Fargo' had been spelled out.

But even stranger things happened. One of Serios' pictures, for instance, showed two storeys of a building and some slight out-of-focus lettering that was, nevertheless, discernible. The building was ultimately acknowledged by the Royal Canadian Mounted Police as one of their Air Division hangars; but they pointed out a curious misspelling, which other observers had also noted. The words in Serios' picture read 'Air Division Cainadain Moun...'

If Serios had somehow used concealed transparencies to produce his pictures, then he was also having to tamper with the originals in an expert way in order to come up with such bizarre images.

Because of such pictures, in which Serios seems to be photographing the past (and distorting reality, too), Eisenbud and fellow researchers arranged an experimental session on 27 May 1967 at the Denver Museum of Natural History where it was hoped his powers might capture on film something that was several thousand years old.

*In*Focus

HIDDEN IN THE HAND?

James Randi, professional stage magician and debunker of things paranormal, has expressed the opinion that Ted Serios is a fraud and that his so-called 'thoughtographs' are produced not by the power of his mind but by means of the device that Serios calls a 'gismo'.

A 'typical Serios gimmick', described by Randi in his book *Flim-flam! – The Truth about Unicorns, Parapsychology and other Delusions*, consists of a small magnifying lens, about ½ inch (1.2 centimetres) in diameter and with a focal length of about 1½ inches (4 centimetres), fixed to one end of a cylinder about 1½ inches (4 centimetres) long. A circle cut from a colour transparency

cylinder
lens
1in (2.5cm)
transparency
½in (1.2cm)

(a 35 mm slide, for example) is glued to the other end of the cylinder. To avoid detection, the device can be wrapped loosely in a tube of paper.

By holding the 'gismo'-lens of a Polaroid camera focused to infinity, and snapping the shutter, the image on the transparency will be thrown on to the Polaroid film. After use, Randi explains, the 'gismo' will slide easily out of the paper (presumably to be disposed of secretly later), and the empty paper tube can be offered to researchers or an audience for inspection.

It is indeed possible to take photographs in this way, although the pictures that result will usually be of poor quality. However, showing how images such as Serios' thoughtographs *could* have been produced is a very different matter from using such an optical device undetected in hundreds of demonstrations. No one to date seems to have done that.

Serios felt confident of success, and began by drawing a mental impression he had received of a man lighting a fire. Strange images were recorded on several of the pictures, the most impressive of which showed a Neanderthal man in a crouching position. But Serios' camera lens had not delved into time to record this image. It was realised immediately by one witness, Professor H. Marie Wormington, of the Department of Anthropology, Colorado College, that it resembled very closely a well-known life-size model of a Neanderthal man group in the Chicago Field Museum of Natural History, postcards of which were readily available.

THE FINAL CURTAIN?

So, did Serios actually fake these photographs? Subsequent studies show that the Neanderthal man in Serios' pictures is shown at different angles; and in the opinion of several professional photographers and photogrammetric engineers, these prints 'could not have been produced from a single microtransparency, but would have required at least several and perhaps eight different ones, most of which could not have been produced from a simple photographic copying of the Field Museum photograph or of a photograph taken by Ted himself'.

Soon after this session, Serios' psychic powers waned for a while and, within a year, although he continued to submit to experiments, all he could produce were 'blackies' or 'whities' without discernible images, leaving psychical researchers still baffled about just what paranormal forces had been at work to produce his former astonishing pictures.

Serios had previously lost his powers at other times – the longest period being for two years – and it seemed to happen without warning. As he put it: 'It is as if a curtain comes down, ker-boom, and that's all, brother'.

But perhaps there *are* warnings, and possibly even symbolic ones, for among the supervised full-frame thoughtographs he produced just prior to losing the 'gift' at one stage was a print which showed the image of a curtain.

THOUGHTS MADE FLESH

APPARITIONS, MANY PEOPLE BELIEVE, EXIST ONLY IN THE HUMAN MIND. BUT WHAT OF THE ART ALLEGEDLY PRACTISED BY TIBETAN ADEPTS – THAT OF MAKING THEIR THOUGHT FORMS MATERIALISE SO STRONGLY THAT THEY CAN ACTUALLY BE SEEN BY OTHER PEOPLE?

Conditions on the road from China to Lhasa, the forbidden capital city of Tibet, were even worse than usual in the winter of 1923 – 1924. Nevertheless, small numbers of travellers, mostly pilgrims wishing to obtain spiritual merit by visiting the holy city and its semi-divine ruler, the Dalai Lama, struggled onwards through the bitter winds and heavy snow. Among them was an elderly woman who appeared to be a peasant from some distant province of the god-king's empire.

The woman was poorly dressed and equipped. Her red woollen skirt and waistcoat, her quilted jacket, and her cap with its lambskin earflaps, were worn and full of holes. From her shoulder hung an ancient leather bag, black with dirt. In this, were the provisions for her journey: barley meal, a piece of dried bacon, a brick of compressed tea, a tube of rancid butter, and a little salt and soda.

With her black hair coated with grease and her dark brown face, she looked like a typical peasant woman. But her hair was really white, dyed with Chinese ink, and her complexion took its colour from oil mixed with cocoa and crushed charcoal. For this Tibetan peasant woman was in reality Alexandra David-Neel, a French woman who, 30 years before, had been an opera singer of note, warmly congratulated by Jules Massenet for her performance in the title role of his opera *Manon*. In the intervening years, Mme David-Neel had travelled to many strange places and had undergone even stranger experiences. These included meeting a magician with the ability to cast spells to hurl flying rice cakes at his enemies, and learning the techniques of *tumo*, an occult art that enables its adepts to sit naked amid the Himalayan snows. Most extraordinary of all, she had constructed, by means of mental and psychic exercises, a *tulpa* – a phantom form born solely from the imagination, and yet so strongly vitalised by the adept's will that it actually becomes visible to other people. A *tulpa* is, to put it another way, an extremely powerful example of what occultists term a thought form.

To understand the nature of the *tulpa*, one has to appreciate that, as far as Tibetan Buddhists (and most Western occultists) are concerned, thought is far more than an intellectual function. Every thought, they believe, affects the 'mind-stuff' that permeates the world of matter, in very much the same way as a stone thrown into a lake makes ripples upon the water's surface. A thought, in other words, produces a 'thought ripple'.

LASTING RIPPLES

Usually thought ripples have only a short life. They decay almost as soon as they are created and make no lasting impression. If, however, the thought is particularly intense, the product of deep passion or fear, or if it is of long duration, the subject of much brooding and meditation, the thought ripple builds into a more permanent thought form, one that has a longer and more intense life.

Tulpas and other thought forms are not considered by Tibetan Buddhists to be 'real' – but neither, according to them, is the world of matter that seemingly surrounds us and appears solid enough. Both are illusory. As a Buddhist classic from the first century AD expresses this firm belief: 'All phenomena are originally in the mind and have really no outward form; therefore, as there is no form, it is an error to think that anything is there. All phenomena merely arise from false notions in the mind. If the mind is independent of these false ideas, then all phenomena disappear.'

If the beliefs about thought forms held by Tibetan Buddhists, mystics and magicians are justified, then many ghostly happenings, hauntings, and cases of localities endowed with a strong 'psychic atmosphere' are easily explained. It seems plausible, for example, that the thought forms created by the violent and passionate mental processes of a murderer, supplemented by the terror stricken emotions of a victim, could linger around the scene of the crime for months, years or even centuries. This could produce intense depression and anxiety in those who visited the 'haunted' spot and, if the thought forms were sufficiently powerful, 'apparitions', such as a re-enactment of the crime, might at times be witnessed by people possessed of psychic sensitivity.

Sometimes, it is even claimed by students of the occult, that those 'spirits' that haunt a particular spot are in fact *tulpas*, thought forms that have been deliberately created by a sorcerer for his own purposes.

The existence of extremely potent thought forms that re-enact the past would, of course, also explain the worldwide reports of visitors to old battlefields 'witnessing' military encounters that took place long before. The sites of the battle of Naseby, which took place during England's Civil War, for instance, and of the 1942 commando raid on Dieppe, are among battlefields that enjoy such ghostly reputations.

A *tulpa* is no more than an extremely powerful thought form, no different in its essential nature from many other ghostly apparitions. Where, however, it does differ from a normal thought form is that it has come into existence, not as a result of an accident, a side-effect of a mental process, but as the result of a deliberate act of will.

The word tulpa is a Tibetan one, but there are adepts in almost every part of the world who believe they are able to manufacture these beings by first drawing together and coagulating some of the mind-stuff of the Universe, and then transferring to it some of their own vitality.

CREATIVE POWER

In Bengal, home of much Indian occultism, the technique is called *kriya shakti* ('creative power'), and is studied and practised by the adepts of Tantrism, a religious magical system concerned with the spiritual aspects of sexuality and numbering both Hindus and Buddhists among its devotees. Initiates of so-called 'left-handed' Tantric cults – that is to say, cults in which men and woman engage in ritual sexual intercourse for mystical and magical purposes – are considered particularly skilled in *kriya shakti*. This is because it is thought that the intense physical and cerebral excitement of the orgasm engenders quite exceptionally vigorous thought forms.

Many Tibetan mystical techniques originated in Bengal, particularly in Bengali Tantrism, and there is a very strong resemblance between the physical, mental and spiritual exercises used by the Tantric yogis of Bengal and the secret inner disciplines of Tibetan Buddhism. It thus seems likely that Tibetans originally derived their theories about *tulpas*, and their methods of creating these strange beings, from Bengali practitioners of *kriya shakti*.

Students of *tulpa* magic begin their training in the art of creating these 'thought beings' by adopting one of the many gods or goddesses of the Tibetan pantheon as a 'tutelary deity' – a sort of patron saint. But while Tibetan initiates regard the gods respectfully, they do not look upon them with any great admiration. For, according to Buddhist belief, although the gods have great powers and are, in a sense 'supernatural', they are just as much slaves of illusion, just as much trapped in the wheel of birth, death, and rebirth, as the humble peasant.

The student retires to a hermitage or other secluded place and meditates on his tutelary deity, known as a *yidam*, for many hours. Here, he combines a contemplation of the spiritual attributes traditionally associated with the *yidam* with visualisation exercises, designed to build up in the mind's eye an image of the *yidam* as portrayed in paintings and statues. To ensure that every waking moment is dedicated to concentrating on the *yidam*, the student continually chants traditional mystic phrases associated with the deity he serves.

PROTECTIVE CIRCLES

He also constructs the *kyilkhors* – literally circles, but actually symbolic diagrams that may be of any shape – believed sacred to his god. Sometimes he will draw these with coloured inks on paper or wood, sometimes he will engrave them on copper or silver, sometimes he will outline them on his floor with coloured powders.

The preparation of the *kyilkhors* must be undertaken with care, for the slightest deviation from the

The rigorous mental and physical discipline taught by Buddhism enables some of its followers, such as the monk seen, below, with drum and incense stick, to attain paranormal powers. In her book Initiations and Initiates in Tibet, *Alexandra David Neel even tells of a man (right, standing on left) who was reputed to be able to hypnotise a subject and cause death at a distance.*

*In*FOCUS

WOLF AT THE DOOR

In her book **Psychic Self Defence,** the occultist Dion Fortune, **left,** related how she once 'formulated a were-wolf accidentally'.

She had this alarming experience while brooding about her feelings of resentment against someone who had hurt her. Lying on her bed, she was thinking of the terrifying wolf-monster of Norse mythology, Fenrir, when suddenly she felt a large grey wolf traditional pattern associated with a particular *yidam* is believed to be extremely dangerous, putting the unwary student in peril of obsession, madness, death, or a stay of thousands of years in one of the hells of Tibetan cosmology.

It is interesting to compare this belief with the idea, strongly held by many Western occultists, that if a magician engaged in evoking a spirit to visible appearance draws his protective magical circle incorrectly, he will be torn in pieces.

Eventually, if the student has persisted with the prescribed exercises, he 'sees' his *yidam*, at first nebulously and briefly, but then persistently and with complete – and sometimes terrifying – clarity.

But this is only the first stage of the process. Meditation, visualisation of the *yidam*, the repetition of spells and contemplation of mystic diagrams is continued until the *tulpa*, in the form of the *yidam*, actually materialises. The devotee can feel the touch of the *tulpa's* feet when he lays his head upon them; he can see the creature's eye following him as he moves about; he can even conduct conversations with it.

THOUGHTS MADE VISIBLE

Eventually, the *tulpa* may be prepared to leave the vicinity of the *kyilkhors* and accompany the devotee on journeys. If the *tulpa* has been fully vitalised, it will by now often be visible to others besides its creator.

Alexandra David-Neel tells how she 'saw' a phantom of this sort which, curiously enough, had not yet become visible to its creator. At the time, Mme David-Neel had developed a great interest in Buddhist art. One afternoon, she was visited by a Tibetan painter who specialised in portraying the 'wrathful deities'. As he approached, she was astonished to see behind him the misty form of one of these much feared and rather unpleasant beings. As she approached the phantom, she stretched out an arm towards it and felt as if she were 'touching a soft object whose substance gave way under the slight push'.

The painter told her that he had for some weeks been engaged in magical rites, calling on the god whose form she had seen, and that he had spent the entire morning painting its picture.

Intrigued by this experience, Mme David-Neel set about making a *tulpa* for herself. To avoid being

Tibetan Buddhists regard their gods, such as the representations above, with reverence but believe that they are no less trapped in the cycles of birth, death and rebirth than any human being. They even attempt to make the gods materialise by a sustained effort of concentration.

influenced by the many Tibetan paintings and images she had seen on her travels, she decided to 'make' not a god or goddess, but a fat, jolly-looking monk whom she could visualise very clearly, and began to concentrate her mind.

She retired to a hermitage, and for some months devoted every waking minute to exercises in concentration and visualisation. Soon she began to get brief glimpses of the monk out of the corner of her eye. He became more solid and lifelike in appearance; and eventually, when she left her hermitage and started on a caravan journey, he included himself in the party, becoming clearly visible and performing actions that she had neither commanded nor consciously expected him to do. He would, for instance, walk and stop to look around him as a traveller might do. Sometimes Mme David-Neel even felt his robe brush against her, and once a hand seemed to touch her shoulder.

Mme David-Neel's *tulpa* eventually began to develop in an unexpected and unwished-for manner. He grew leaner, his expression became malignant, and he was 'troublesome and bold'. One day, a herdsman, who brought Mme David-Neel a present of some butter, saw the *tulpa* in her tent, and mistook it for a real monk. It had got out of control. Indeed, her creation turned into what she called a 'day-nightmare' and she decided to get rid of it. Eventually it took her six months of concentrated effort and meditation to do so.

If this, and many similar stories told in Tibet, are to be believed, the creation of a *tulpa* is not a matter to be undertaken lightly. It is, in fact, yet another fascinating example of the remarkable powers of the human mind.

materialise beside her, and was aware of its body pressing against hers.

From her reading about thought forms, Fortune knew she must gain control of the beast immediately. So she dug her elbow into its hairy ribs and pushed the creature off the bed. The animal disappeared through the wall.

The story was not yet over, however, for another member of the household said she had seen the eyes of the wolf in the corner of her room. Dion Fortune realised she must destroy the creature. Summoning the beast, she saw a thin thread joining it to her and began to imagine she was drawing the life out of the beast along this thread. The wolf faded to a formless grey mass, and ceased to exist.

The capacity of the human mind to create thoughts so powerful that their forms are visible has long been attested to by mystic religions. Here, we present a collection of pictures that suggest that this capacity indeed exists – casual photographs that include strange figures which no one saw at the time, and seemingly produced by mind-power alone

'Thoughts are things', insisted Annie Besant and C.W. Leadbeater in their book *Thought Forms.* The appearance of the thought form was believed to be the outcome of three factors: the quality of the thought determined the colour, the nature of the thought determined the shape, and the so-called 'definiteness' of the thought determined the clarity of the outline. The thought form of a person 'not terrified but seriously startled', for instance, was represented, as shown *above,* by an 'onrush' of crescent-shaped forms. The colours are the 'livid grey' of fear, which almost immediately becomes tinged with the red of anger as 'the man is already partially recovering from the shock, and beginning to be angry'. Another example, *right,* represents a conscious attempt to feel love and sympathy for mankind – and is the result of an attempt to imagine those feelings pouring forth 'in the six directions' of Hindu mystical thought. Everyone, Besant and Leadbeater believed, is sensitive to thought forms, even if not everyone can actually see them. In this way, one's thoughts, even those that remain unspoken, have a constant, if subtle, influence on other people. 'It is thus evident', Besant and Leadbeater concluded, 'that every man who thinks along high lines is doing missionary work, even though he may be entirely unconscious of it'.

The photograph, *above,* was taken by London medium Gladys Hayter, and is of her daughter, Dawn, driving the new car she had given her in March 1979. When the film was developed in September of the same year, both women were astonished to see on the print something that neither of them had been aware of at the time – the head of a small, blonde girl who was apparently sitting on the back seat of the car as evident in the enlargement, *right.* So who was the mystery girl? In a sitting with the direct voice medium Leslie Flint, Mrs Hayter's mother 'spoke', asking Gladys what she thought of the photograph and going on to observe that the girl,whose name was Sheila, was a happy little child who had attached herself to the direct voice medium's circle, of which Gladys herself was a member. 'Well, she's a nice little thing, of course,' commented Gladys' mother, 'but you know she's nothing to do with our family ... She's a little girl who's been coming round and playing, can you hear me?' In a later sitting, a spirit named Samantha Rigg-Milner revealed that the little girl's surname was Wilkins. 'I know the – I know who the little girl – I have seen her, you know ... Sheila – I have seen her in the car in your picture; I am very friendly with her.'

Mrs Hayter herself was convinced that the face of a Golden Labrador dog can be seen between Dawn and the ghostly child. This, she suggests, is Brandy, a dog that belonged to her daughter and was killed at the age of 18 months in 1974. The dog was also apparently a member of the medium's circle – and Gladys' mother confirmed that 'the dog is often around' in the afterworld.

The picture of a pleasant tea party on a summer lawn, *above,* was taken by Arthur Springer, a retired police inspector, in his own garden at Tingewick, Buckinghamshire, England, in 1916. Allegedly, no one was aware of the presence of the dog on the left-hand side of the picture until the film was developed.

Although, unlike human figures, spirit photographs of animals have proved remarkably difficult to capture in the studio, ghostly figures of animals do sometimes appear in photographs taken by amateurs – generally, as here, without having been seen by the photographer at the time. Often they are later recognised as dead pets of which the photographer, or someone else who was present when the picture was taken, was very fond. Indeed, it has been conjectured that these ghostly images on the film are actually conjured up by the intensity of emotion that was felt for the dead animal. The women at the tea table in this particular picture are clearly happily unaware of the presence of anything as weird or disarming as a phantom dog. But if the photographer was unaware that the ghostly dog was there, why would he have chosen to set his camera up in such a way as to frame it perfectly? If he did not see it, as he claimed, the shot is a curiously asymmetrical one, with the women unnaturally grouped to the right of the picture. Was the photographer perhaps surreptitiously leaving space to add a fake dog when he developed the film in his laboratory? The fact is that the original photograph was 'cropped' to give the picture, as reproduced *above,* and the group at the table was positioned centrally in the original composition.

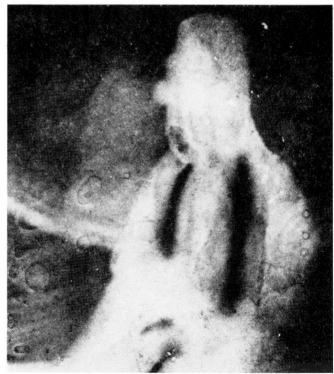

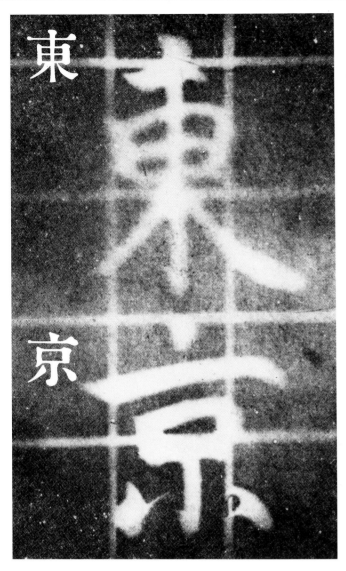

The thoughtographic image, *above,* was produced under the supervision of Professor Fukurai on 10 May 1911 by the psychic Mrs Sadako Takahashi. Under hypnosis, a secondary personality emerged to give this information: 'The picture . . . was my thoughtography ... I wanted to give the warning that one should not be tempted by personal profit.' On 10 February 1917, Mr Kohichi Mita, a stage magician, produced the two plates, *below,* at a public experiment in the city of Nagoya. Separately, the two plates did not make any sense; but together, remarkably, they formed two Japanese characters.

Between 1910 and 1913, Professor T. Fukurai of the Imperial University, Tokyo, president of the Psychical Institute of Japan, conducted a remarkable series of experiments in clairvoyance and thoughtography with a number of Japanese psychics. Among those whom he investigated extensively was a Mrs Ikuko Nagao, who became aware of her psychic abilities after the death of her small son. Mrs Nagao was spectacularly successful in clairvoyance, as well as thoughtography experiments, which she was asked to produce images on sealed photographic plates. Like many psychics, she was able to produce impressions of objects. The picture, *left,* for instance, is a thoughtographic image of a figure from a Buddhist religious scroll. Even more remarkable, however, was her ability to produce accurate impressions of Japanese characters. Critics objected that the figures could be produced equally well by exposing the plate through a piece of pasteboard or similar material with the shape of the letter cut out of it. The example, *above,* of two particularly complex characters, was made to show how difficult such faking would have been. In any event, the phenomena were, of course, produced in the presence of expert witnesses.

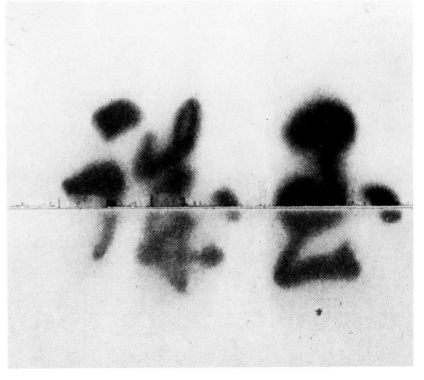

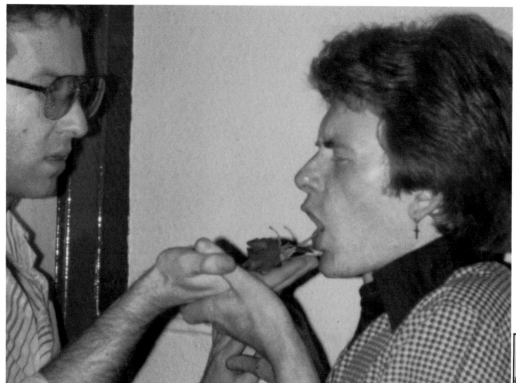

OUT OF THIN AIR

FLOWERS, FRUIT, ORNAMENTS AND EVEN LIVE ANIMALS HAVE SUPPOSEDLY BEEN MATERIALISED THROUGH SOME ESPECIALLY GIFTED MEDIUMS. THE PRODUCTION OF SUCH OBJECTS, CALLED 'APPORTS', IS SURROUNDED BY MUCH CONTROVERSY – AND SOMETIMES THE CRY OF 'FRAUD'

Former medium Paul McElhoney, top, seems to be producing an apport of a fresh flower from his mouth. There were no signs that it had been regurgitated. Flower apports, above, were not all that allegedly appeared at his demonstrations. The cast metal model of Cologne Cathedral, right, landed in the palm of SPR council member Anita Gregory 'from nowhere'. Ceros, McElhoney's spirit guide said it was a gift from her dead father. Mrs Gregory discovered later that her father had spent his honeymoon in a hotel overlooking Cologne Cathedral.

The problem about those who claim to produce apports is seen in the case of one-time London medium, Paul McElhoney, who frequently held demonstrations at his home in the 1970s and 80s. Like many mediums, he performed his apport-producing displays in a darkened room – something that would normally arouse the suspicions of believers as well as non-believers.

In McElhoney's case, however, several observers reported that flowers did indeed appear to have apported from his mouth. In November 1981, spiritualist Michael Cleary told *Psychic News* of an experience he had at the medium's home circle. He said he had searched McElhoney and the seance room before the proceedings began. During the seance, the medium was entranced by a spirit called Ceros. 'When Ceros brought the first flowers, the lights were on,' said Cleary. 'I looked into Paul's mouth. There was nothing there. Then a [fresh] flower began to fall from his mouth. Carnations are very significant in my family. I had previously asked my mother in the spirit world to bring that kind of flower. When Ceros aported a carnation for me, he said it was a present from a woman in the spirit world.'

Another witness to this phenomenon was author and investigator Guy Lyon Playfair, who also received a carnation. When home, he put it in his mouth and tried to talk as the medium had done. 'The stalk stuck in my throat. I nearly threw up. Paul talked easily and then produced the carnation.'

Although Cleary said he had searched the medium and the room before McElhoney began his demonstration, he failed to look in the tape-recorder which McElhoney was using. During one demonstration, a reporter – determined to establish the truth – switched on the light and found a bunch of flowers inside the recorder itself. It was a discovery that marked the end of McElhoney's career.

PLANTED FLOWERS?

Flowers have been common apports for well over 150 years. One of the earliest investigators of this phenomenon was a Frenchman, Dr G. P. Billot, who witnessed the production of flower apports by a blind woman medium way back in October 1820.

One of the most extraordinary accounts of an apport concerns a famous English medium, Madame d'Esperance, in whose presence a materialised spirit named Yolande was said to appear. At a seance in 1880, Yolande took a glass carafe that had been half-filled with sand and water and placed it in the centre of the room, covering it with a thin piece of drapery. The sitters then watched in amazement as the drapery began rising and Yolande came out of the cabinet, in which Madame d'Esperance was seated, to inspect what was happening. When she removed the drapery, it was seen that a perfect plant had grown in minutes.

Yolande told the sitters to sing quietly for a few minutes; and when they inspected the plant again, they found it had burst into bloom, with a flower 5 inches (12.5 centimetres) in diameter. It had a thick woody stem, which filled the neck of the carafe, was 22 inches (56 centimetres) high and had 29 leaves. It was subsequently identified as a native of India, *Ixora crocata,* and lasted for three months.

Madame d'Esperance, right, was one of the foremost physical mediums of the late 19th century. She is seen with the golden lily that – through the agency of her materialised guide Yolande – literally grew in front of her sitters on 28 June 1890 to a height of 7 feet (2 metres). Exuding a strong fragrance and with five flowers in bloom, it seemed solid enough – yet at her next seance, Yolande dematerialised it in seven minutes. All that remained was this photograph and a couple of the flowers.

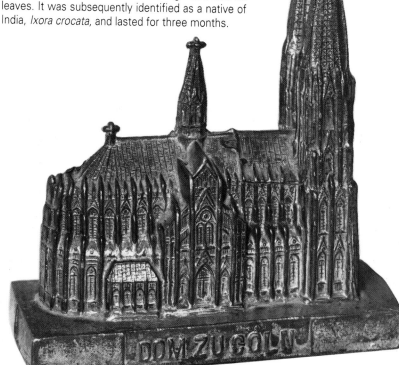

Ten years later, the same medium was responsible for an equally spectacular apport. This time – on 28 June 1890 – a beautiful golden lily with an overpowering perfume grew before the eyes of the sitters to a height of 7 feet (2 metres). Five of its 11 flowers were in full bloom; and in photographs taken at the time, it was seen to tower above the medium. Yolande told the sitters, however, that it could not remain and became quite upset when she found she could not dematerialise it. She asked them to keep the plant in a darkened room until the next session, on 5 July, when it was placed in the centre of the room. Its physical presence was recorded at 9.23 p.m., but by 9.30 p.m. it had vanished. The only proof of its existence were the photographs and a couple of the flowers.

Even with such large apports, more hardened sceptics could probably suggest ways in which they might have been produced fraudulently. But fraud is difficult to accept in cases where mediums materialise items at the request of sitters. A friend of Agnes Nichols (later, Mrs Samuel Guppy), one of the most gifted apport mediums during the 1860s and 1870s, once asked for a sunflower, and the medium complied with its immediate production, in a darkened seance room. It was a 6 foot (1.6-metre) specimen, which arrived on a table with a mass of earth around its roots. At another seance, each sitter was asked to name a fruit or vegetable: the apports that were received included a banana, two oranges, a bunch of white grapes, a bunch of black grapes, a cluster of filberts, three walnuts, a dozen damsons, a slice of candied pineapple, three figs, two apples, an onion, a peach, a few almonds, three dates, a potato, two large pears, a pomegranate, two crystallised greengages, a pile of dried currants, a lemon and a large bunch of raisins.

Doves and other birds are as popular with apport mediums as they are with magicians, but their materialisation is achieved under very different conditions. An Australian boot-maker, Charles Bailey, is even credited with apporting an entire menagerie during his many years as a medium. To rule out trickery, he allowed himself to be stripped, searched and dressed in clothes supplied by investigators. Dr C. W. McCarthy, an eminent medical man in Sydney, imposed even more stringent test conditions. Having searched Bailey, he then placed the medium in a sack with holes for his hands, and tied him up.

On occasions, the sitters were searched as well and the medium would be placed inside a cage covered with mosquito netting. The door to the room was locked or sealed, the fireplace was blocked and paper pasted over the window. The only furniture allowed in the room was a table and chairs for the sitters. Yet, after a few minutes of darkness, when the lights were put on, Bailey was found to be holding apports, such as two nests with a live bird in each. At other seances, he produced a live, 18-inch (46-centimetre), shovel-nosed shark and a crab dripping in seaweed. Many of the live apports produced at his seances disappeared as mysteriously as they had arrived.

Later in his career, however, Bailey's mediumship was found to be far from convincing by a number of investigators who produced evidence to show that he had purchased the 'apports' from animal dealers. But others remained entirely convinced that some, even if not all of his phenomena were genuine.

STOLEN ITEMS?

Intriguingly, the 'spirit control' of a famous medium, Mrs Everitt, refused to produce apports. 'I do not approve of bringing them,' she explained cryptically, 'for they are generally stolen.' There have certainly been well-corroborated cases where an apport has been an object that has been dematerialised from one place and rematerialised in another, sometimes at a sitter's request. The following account was written by Ernesto Bozzano, an eminent Italian psychical researcher:

'In March, 1904, in a sitting in the house of Cavaliere Peretti, in which the medium was an

The American medium Keith Milton Rhinehart, above, held public demonstrations in London in the 1960s, which provoked a guarded reaction from some of the audience. He produced numerous objects, above right, from his mouth, including a prickly sea horse; but there is some evidence to suggest that he had merely regurgitated them.

Two frames from a controversial films taken at Rolla, Missouri USA, below, allegedly show the paranormal movement of objects through the glass wall of a minilab. Despite several years of research, none of the minilab pioneers has managed to induce PK on a scale comparable to that of the physical mediums.

intimate friend of ours, gifted with remarkable physical mediumship, and with whom apports could be obtained at command, I begged the communicating spirit to bring me a small block of pyrites which was lying on my writing table about two kilometres [1.2 miles] away. The spirit replied (through the medium) that the power was almost exhausted but that all the same he would make the attempt.

'Soon after, the medium sustained the usual spasmodic twitchings which signified the arrival of an apport, but without our hearing the fall of any object on the table or floor. We asked for an explanation from the spirit operator, who informed us that although he had managed to disintegrate a portion of the object desired, and had brought it into the room, there was not enough power for him to ... re-integrate it.

'He added, "Light the light". We did so, and found, to our great surprise, that the table, the clothes and hair of the sitters, as well as the furniture and carpets of the room, were covered with the thinnest layer of brilliant impalpable pyrites. When I returned home after the sitting, I found the little block of pyrites lying on my writing table from which a large fragment, about one third of the whole piece, was missing.'

Apport mediums seem to use different psychic techniques to produce the phenomenon; but, with some, the object seems to materialise out of their bodies. T. Lynn, a miner from the north of England, was photographed producing apports in this way. Small ectoplasmic shapes were often seen extending from his body, usually near the solar plexus. Hewat McKenzie and Major C. Mowbray tested Lynn at the British College of Psychic Science, London, in 1928. The medium was put in a bag, and his hands were tied to his knees with tapes. Flashlight photographs taken by the investigators showed luminous connections between his body and the apports.

Another miner, Jack Webber, was photographed some years later producing an apport in a similar way. Webber, a Welshman, was famous as a physical medium at whose seances trumpets would levitate and spirit voices would speak to those present. At a seance in 1938, Webber was searched thoroughly by a policeman in front of all

the sitters, and then tied to a chair. This account of the seance is taken from Harry Edwards' book, *The Mediumship of Jack Webber:*

'The red light was on, sufficiently bright for all to see the medium with his arms bound to the chair. Trumpets were in levitation ... one of these turned round, presenting its large opening to the solar plexus region and an object was heard to fall into it. It then came to the author who was asked to take out of the trumpet the article within – an Egyptian ornament. After a minute or two, the trumpet again travelled to the solar plexus and another object was heard to fall into it.'

In November of the same year, at a seance in Paddington, London, Webber's guide announced his intention of trying to materialise a brass ornament from an adjoining room. He asked for a photograph to be taken at a particular moment and said that this ought to record the production of the

The Indian guru Sai Baba, above left, worshipped as a modern Hindu saint, holds one of his many apports.

The ex-miner Jack Webber, above, produces a cord-like string of ectoplasm from his mouth. On several occasions, small ornaments, top, were seen to take shape in a white cloud over his solar plexus; but when handled, they were perfectly solid.

apport. The sitters then heard the sound of an object falling to the floor. When the plate was developed, the small ornament – a bird weighing 2 ounces (57 grams) – could be seen apparently emerging in a white substance from the medium's solar plexus.

❚❚ AT OTHER SEANCES, BAILEY PRODUCED A LIVE SHARK AND A CRAB DRIPPING IN SEAWEED. MANY OF THE LIVE APPORTS PRODUCED AT HIS SEANCES DISAPPEARED AS MYSTERIOUSLY AS THEY ARRIVED. ❚❚

American medium, Keith Milton Rhinehart, demonstrated apport mediumship in London in the 1960s at the Caxton Hall. In a well-lit area, before a capacity audience, he successfully produced a number of items from his mouth, including a very prickly sea-horse. Semi-precious stones were also 'apported' through his body: they were found embedded in his skin and were plucked out by witnesses. Some members of the audience, however, were distinctly unimpressed: the stones were never seen to emerge through his skin, they claimed, and seemed to have been deliberately implanted in his flesh. Similarly, a number of witnesses thought some of his supposed apports had merely been regurgitated.

But a comparison of the best apport mediums does provide some striking similarities, and some believe that this indicates that it is a genuine phenomenon. At the turn of the century, Henry Sausse recorded many instances of apports produced by an entranced woman medium. Her method was to form her hands into a cup, in full light. A small cloud would then be seen to form inside. This would transform itself instantly into an apport, such as a spray of roses, complete with flowers, buds and leaves. There are countless similar stories of physical mediumship; but the fact remains that apports are rare today.

FOR MOST PEOPLE, A VISIT TO THE DENTIST MEANS STARK WAITING ROOMS, THE SOUND OF THE ELECTRIC DRILL AND THE TASTE OF ANTISEPTIC MOUTHWASH. BUT FOR PATIENTS ATTENDING FOR PSYCHIC DENTISTRY, THINGS COULD BE RATHER DIFFERENT

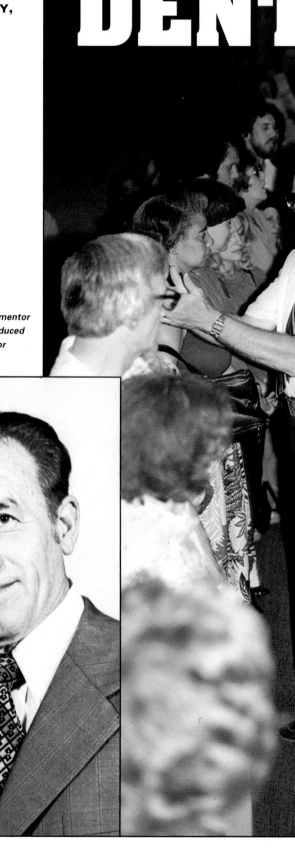

O f all the healing gifts, that of psychic dentistry is surely the most bizarre and the most difficult to explain. The few mediums who practise it are said to be able to mend bad teeth instantly with gold, silver or porcelain fillings that materialise in their patients' mouths. Sometimes, it is claimed, new teeth even grow where previously there had been only blackened stumps.

Such astonishing statements have their share of critics: even many believers in the paranormal treat psychic dentistry with some suspicion. But few who witnessed evangelist Willard Fuller at work remained sceptical. He is even said to have produced 'mouth miracles' in over 25,000 patients.

Fuller, an American, graduated in business administration and gained a degree in electrical engineering before the Baptist Church beckoned. Then, with another degree under his belt, this time in theology, he set out to travel across the United States. For 10 years, he preached as an evangelist for the Baptist Church.

Two things then happened that were to alter his life radically: he was excommunicated – he claimed, for asking too many questions – and, at about the same time, he went through what the old-time Pentacostalists called a 'baptism of the Holy Spirit'. Shortly afterwards, in response to his calling, he embarked on a healing mission.

To begin with, he practised spiritual healing that was no different from any other. But what started out as simply the laying on of hands was to develop into something quite extraordinary when Fuller met up with A. C. McKaig. Fuller already knew of this man who prayed for people's 'dental needs', with the frequent result that their cavities were miraculously filled. So, when he heard that McKaig was preaching in Shreveport, Louisiana, he had no hesitation in going along in order to witness the service for himself.

Fuller watched with growing excitement as the healer treated a variety of illnesses; but the best was yet to come, for McKaig had saved his dental treatments until last. One of those in the audience was a woman who had never visited a dentist in her life. She had a cavity that badly needed attention. Fuller watched as McKaig placed his hands on the woman's head and prayed for God to help her. The healer then gave her a torch and a hand-mirror so she could look inside her own mouth. As she examined her tooth, she gave a shriek of delight. 'It has silver in it!' she shouted. Fuller was standing nearby. He rushed over to the woman and peered at the filled tooth. 'It was bright, shiny and looking like a newly-minted coin,' he declared.

The Reverend A. C. McKaig, below, was Willard Fuller's mentor and the man who first introduced him to the idea of praying for people's dental needs.

PSY DENT

HIC STRY

The 18th-century drawing, below, shows a tooth being pulled and the patient's neck simultaneously being put out of joint. Fortunately, things have changed since then: but a visit to a conventional modern dentist's surgery, bottom, can still fill many people with undue terror.

Further such miracles were to follow as McKaig treated a stream of people, but one of the strangest happenings was reserved for Fuller himself. Abruptly, McKaig turned to him, pointed and announced: 'Now I am going to pray for you and ask God to bless you'. The healer was a small man and he had to mount a two-step platform in order to be at Fuller's height. The scene may have looked incongruous enough, but the results were apparently immediate and dramatic. God, says Fuller, spoke

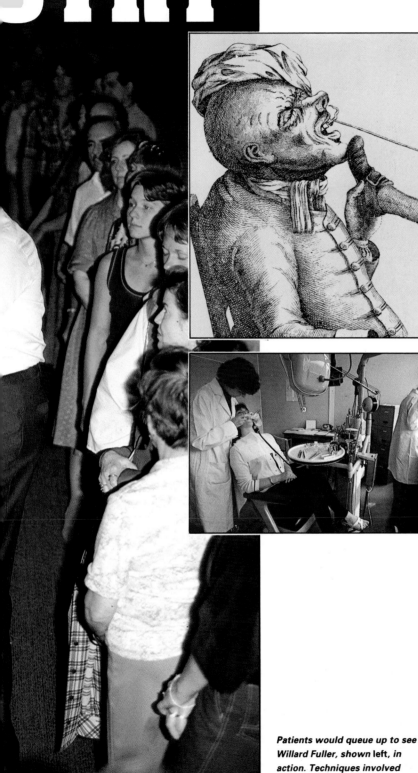

Patients would queue up to see Willard Fuller, shown left, in action. Techniques involved smacking the patient on both cheeks – the only painful part of an otherwise pain-free experience.

to him in the following words, words he has never forgotten: 'Think it not strange, my son, all the things that thou has seen me do through him, this, my servant. For all the things that thou hast seen me do through him, I shall do through thee, and greater things I shall do through thee than thou hast seen me do through him.' It was enough to inspire Fuller and set him on the road to psychic dentistry.

Fuller admitted that it took some time before he found the courage to introduce it into his own healing services, since he was concerned as to whether it worked for him the way it had worked for his mentor. When he finally met the challenge, by treating a young man for a cavity, he was overjoyed to discover that he did indeed possess the power to heal. After that first tentative beginning, Fuller did not look back.

Bryce Bond, an American writer and healer, witnessed the psychic dentist at work. As he explained: 'Fuller's technique is simple. He gently smacks the person on both cheeks at the same time and says: "In the name of Jesus, be thou whole".' It is believed possible that the moment of intense belief is able to produce a spiritual alchemy in which gold, silver or porcelain take shape inside the patients' mouths. It may seem unlikely, but there are many prepared to testify that they have seen it taking place.

Those who have witnessed a filling form describe it as a small, bright spot that becomes larger until it fills the whole cavity, rather like a speeded-up picture of a rose blooming. The British psychic Matthew Manning endorses this description.

When he attended one of Fuller's healing sessions in New York, Manning was cynical to begin with; but, once he had witnessed the phenomenon at first-hand, he felt convinced enough to declare the treatment 'absolutely genuine'. He reported what he saw to *Psychic News:* 'One woman had at the back of her jaw a very decayed tooth which was black. I saw it fill with something white which appeared to be a kind of ceramic substance. When finished, she had a new white tooth. Several people were peering into the woman's mouth. The substance came from her gum. I saw this happen.'

Few doctors, however, were prepared to take Fuller's claims seriously, though some witnessed his sessions for themselves. Scientists employed by NASA at Cape Kennedy were among a group who received dental healings during a meeting in Miami, Florida, and doctors were present among the 400 witnesses who attended a demonstration at Wagner College, Staten Island, New York. One

substance; others talk of a platinum-coloured metal being used. But neither substance has been subjected to scientific analysis.

Fuller took time off from his ministry to train another psychic dentist, Paul Esch. Bryce Bond also investigated Esch's abilities and described his skills as nothing short of 'a miracle'. Of one meeting he attended in Woodstock, New York – a year before he encountered Fuller – Bond said: 'One of those present had a few empty spaces in her mouth, she tasted blood, then a tooth broke through the surface of the empty gum. Almost all those present noticed their teeth became whiter.'

Apparently, certain members of the group received two or three gold fillings. The sessions are very similar to Fuller's. Bond went on to say: 'The only way to believe it is to see it happen first-hand.' Perhaps he should have also added that the only way to see it happen is to *believe* it could happen, since faith is said to play a large part in both psychic dentistry and healing generally.

Fuller is shown, left, *shining a torch into a patient's mouth, while the patient examines his new 'miracle' filling. Fuller's wife, looking on, seems as surprised as anyone.*

Fuller would use none of the paraphernalia of the modern dentist, but carried the tools of his trade around with him. A look inside his briefcase, below, *reveals that his only concession to technology is a battery for use in his torch.*

Swedish doctor, however, was prepared to speak out. Dr Audrey Kargere from the Humanist College, Stockholm, was 'highly elated' when several of her silver fillings were transformed to gold. She also benefited from Fuller's more conventional healing, which resulted in her badly swollen leg returning to normal very rapidly. Peter Williams was another doctor at the same session. He was said to have been delighted, but baffled, when a blackened tooth was transformed to 'bright, shiny gold'.

MYSTERIOUS SUBSTANCES

According to Bryce Bond, it was not even necessary to ask for Fuller's help to benefit from the healing; it was enough to be present at one of the meetings. During the session he attended, he did not volunteer for psychic dentistry. Despite this, throughout the meeting, he was aware of a tingling in his gums, followed by numbness. Later, he discovered small pieces of tartar (the hard chalky deposit that the dentist scrapes off during a routine clean up) had become dislodged, and he was able to pick the small granules off his tongue.

Apart from claims that silver fillings have turned to gold, less conventional materials have sometimes been said to fill the cavities. Some witnesses claim seeing teeth filled with a translucent ruby-like

Stephen Turoff is one of Britain's foremost psychic surgeons. A carpenter by training, he has no medical knowledge, yet claims to cure a host of illnesses while possessed by the spirit of a mid-19th century German doctor

THE HEALING SPIRIT

I realised I had a gift for healing when I was in my early 20s. At that time, strange things began happening to me. I started to see things other people couldn't see. I heard voices that other people couldn't hear. I could see colours around people and around objects. But I told no one about it until my mid-20s because it started to get quite bad. I really didn't know what was happening to me.

These voices were very real...both inside and outside my head. It was quite weird. I then went to a spiritualist meeting and the medium there said: 'You have the gift of healing and this will eventually manifest itself.' This gave me a direction that allowed me to channel my powers into something very positive and very beautiful. At that time, I was healing by the laying on of hands. I didn't give up my carpentry career, though. At first, I saw only about ten to 15 people a week, but that wasn't enough to make a living. Gradually it built up.

Dr Kahn [Turoff's 'spirit doctor'] first came through to me a few years ago. I think it was 1 July 1985, and it changed the course of my life. I remember him taking me over and operating on a patient – a woman who had an ovarian cyst and who was in great pain. After I came back to myself [Turoff rarely remembers what has happened during his trances], I thought, 'My God, what's going on?' But the result was that the woman was out of pain. When she went back to hospital, they also found the cyst had completely gone.

For that operation, Dr Kahn didn't use any instruments. He seemed to do it with my finger. He gave the woman an invisible injection – no one could see it, but she felt it. As he ran my finger up her stomach, she felt it open and a hand move inside her. Don't ask me how, I don't know.

Not all psychic operations take place in this way. Some are more physical. Sometimes, Dr Kahn cuts the body open and will go inside. But sometimes, it's more of an 'etheric' operation. He lays a knife on the skin and people actually feel it going into them – although the blade doesn't penetrate the body at all. It seems that Dr Kahn extends and solidifies the etheric – an invisible forcefield – surrounding the blade, and it is this that cuts into the person.

Sometimes I'll have my hands on somebody and they'll suddenly say: 'I can feel movement in my stomach, there's a pair of hands in my stom-

In the surgery of his home in Danbury, Essex, psychic surgeon Stephen Turoff operates on a patient while possessed by the spirit of Dr Kahn.

> **" THERE'S NO PHYSICAL ANAESTHETIC. INSTEAD, THERE'S AN ENERGY FIELD AROUND THE BED THAT SEEMS TO ANAESTHETISE PATIENTS WITHOUT ACTUALLY MAKING THEM UNCONSCIOUS — A KIND OF STERILISED ZONE. "**

ach.' There may be a bit of discomfort, but otherwise hardly anything.

When Kahn does open the body, it's usually only a minor cut. We call him 'the keyhole surgeon' because he makes a little incision and goes in with a prong – it's so simple. In other operations, we've had lumps the size of golf balls come out of people's mouths. He's also gone straight up nasal passages with a six-inch knife to cut out growths.

I don't use any physical anaesthetic. Instead, there's an energy field around the bed that seems to anaesthetise patients, without actually making them unconscious. It's an area where bacteria cannot form – a kind of sterilised zone. It's within that area that Dr Khan and his colleagues work [some 15 spirit doctors – including three nurses – form a back-up team].

We've had people cured of cancer instantaneously. We know because they report back. One woman who came here had cervical cancer. She came here once, went back to the hospital and they couldn't find any trace of it. Another guy had a tumour on the spine. They gave him a few months to live, but they couldn't operate because it was so embedded. I saw him once only; and when he went to the hospital for a check-up and X-rays, they found the tumour was gone.

People also come for spiritual and psychological problems, but most come for physical ailments. I can't prescribe drugs because I'm not a doctor. But Dr Kahn does suggest at times a health pill – like a vitamin – or a diet. He speaks to my wife who writes it down; she's generally in the room with me. I can occasionally hear him talk to her; sometimes it's clear, at other times it sounds a bit crackly.

To call up Dr Kahn, I send a thought out and ask him to come. Sometimes, another spirit doctor will take me over if Dr Kahn can't be there, but that's only happened about three or four times. He [Kahn] says he doesn't work for anyone else because it's taken so long to blend in with me.

Although Kahn is from the 19th century, he has progressed in medical techniques. Not only is he dematerialising tumours, for example, he's also dematerialising actual organs of the body. If they're too infected and can't be cured, he takes them out. In these cases, there's no blood.

The last dematerialisation was done on a matron from a hospital; she had secondary cancer of the Fallopian tube and left ovary. She was in here for only a few minutes, but the next day, while in hospital for examination, they discovered that the ovary and tube were gone. The surgeon – a friend of hers – phoned her that night and said that he had gone through all her records, scans and X-rays, and while he accepted the cancer might have disappeared, he just couldn't understand how organs could vanish.

Sometimes when healing, we rub water on to a person's skin. Then he [Kahn] puts a white towel on the person and places my hands on top of it. For some reason, that heals. When he puts my hands above the towel, you can often see a pink ray coming from them on to the towel. Sometimes, the ray is blue or mauve, but generally it's pink.

I've tried to let people see what we do and formulate their own opinions. I've even done a demonstration in Spain in front of 300 doctors. We've also had doctors come here to watch me work. They've conversed with Dr Kahn; they've seen patients get better. Of course, I can't cure everybody, but we get a very high percentage.

I'm conscious of a divine love – a spark or power – coming through me. I haven't got to see the patients, but it's a part of my life and I love it. To be honest with you, it is my life; and if I had to pack it up, it would break my heart.

A case of a glowing human who was otherwise healthy comes from a letter to the *English Mechanic* of 24 September 1869:

'An American lady, on going to bed, found that a light was issuing from the upper side of the fourth toe on her right foot. Rubbing increased the phosphorescent glow and it spread up her foot. Fumes were also given off, making the room disagreeable; and both light and fumes continued when the foot was held in a basin of water. Even washing with soap could not dim the toe. It lasted for three-quarters of an hour before fading away, and was witnessed by her husband.'

When it comes to luminescent animals, such as glow worms and fireflies, the scientific explanation is that they light up as a result of chemical reactions involving oxygen, luciferase, luciferin and adenosine triphosphate (ATP) within the body. But this kind of chemical reaction has not been offered as the reason for the human glow.

Many mystics and occultists maintain that every human being is surrounded by light – or an aura – of varying colours, which can be seen after occult training or by natural clairvoyance. The strength of this light is said to vary with each individual, but is supposed to be brightest around those whose spiritual nature is most developed, or those who are in

HUMAN GLOW-WORMS

A blue glow emanated from Anna Morana's breasts as she lay asleep. It happened regularly for several weeks, and each time the luminescence lasted for several seconds. No one could explain it.

An asthma sufferer, living in Italy, she first started to glow during an attack in 1934, and she became a news sensation for a time as the 'luminous woman of Pirano'. The blue light that she gave off was recorded on film, and was also witnessed by many doctors. One psychiatrist said that it was caused by 'electrical and magnetic organisms in the woman's body developed in eminent degree,' which did little to clarify the matter. Another doctor speculated that she had an abnormally high level of sulphides in her blood because of her weak condition and also because of her fasting, inspired by religious zeal. These sulphides, he said, were stimulated into luminescence by a natural process of ultra-violet radiation. Even if this were true, it did not explain why the glow came just from the breasts, and always only while the woman slept.

Data on 'glowing' humans is found in medical literature, as well as religious writings and folklore. Many toxicology textbooks discuss 'luminous wounds', for instance, and in their encyclopedic collection of *Anomalies and Curiosities of Medicine*, Dr George Gould and Dr Walter Pyle described a case of breast cancer that produced a light from the sore that was sufficiently strong to illuminate the hands of a watch which was lying several feet away. Hereward Carrington (1881-1958), an American psychical researcher, also told of a child whose body, after death from acute indigestion, was surrounded by a strange blue glow.

As she lay on her death-bed, above, a celestial light in the form of a cross and stars were seen to glow around the corpse of Jane Pallister, who died in 1833. Her son and other witnesses attributed this wonder to her extreme virtue.

Two wingless, female common European glow-worms, right, send out a cold, greenish-yellow light from an organ in the tail-end of their abdomens. These glow-worms (in fact, beetles of the family Lampyridae*) produce light by means of a chemical reaction, and use it to attract males during the mating season.*

During Christ's transfiguration on the mountain, depicted above right, his garments became white and shining as light – a phenomenon portrayed here by the round and angular shapes surrounding him. Light features again in the conversion of Paul on the road to Damascus, illustrated far right, when a brilliant flash seemed to knock him from his horse: we are told that it came from a vision of Jesus.

mystics distinguished four different types of aura: the nimbus, the halo, the aureola and the glory. The nimbus and halo stream from or surround the head, and the aureola emanates from the whole body. The glory, meanwhile, is an intensified form of the whole-body glow – a veritable flooding of light.

Theosophists speak of five auras: the health aura, the vital aura, the Karmic aura, the aura of character, and the aura of spiritual nature. Various colours of aural light are also said to indicate differing emotional states or character. Brilliant red means anger and force; dirty red, passion and sensuality; brown, avarice; rose, affection; yellow, intellectual activity; purple, spirituality; blue, religious devotion; green, deceit or, in a deeper shade, sympathy. The Polish medium Stefan Ossowiecki, in the early 1900s, occasionally saw a particularly dark aura that indicated the approach of death.

NATURAL FLAMES

Most people are familiar with the Christian representation of the halo. It is less known, however, that the original purpose of the crowns and distinctive head-dresses worn by kings and priests was to symbolise the halo. Representations of the aureola around great teachers and the holy are found in virtually every culture: they occur, for example, in places as far apart as Peru, Mexico, Egypt, Sri Lanka, India and Japan.

Pope Benedict XIV, in his great treatise on beatification and canonisation, wrote:

'It seems to be a fact that there are natural flames which at times visibly encircle the human head, and also that, from a man's whole person, fire may on occasion radiate naturally – not, however, like a flame which streams upwards, but rather in the form of sparks which are given off all round; further, that some people become resplendent with a blaze of light, though this is not inherent in themselves, but attaches rather to their clothes, or to the staff or to the spear they are carrying.'

Stories are legion in the hagiographical records of priests who illuminated dark cells and chapels with a light that emanated from their bodies or, conversely, seemed to stream upon them from some mysterious source. When the 14th-century Carthusian monk, John Tornerius, failed to appear in time to celebrate the first mass, the sacristan who went to fetch him found that his cell was radiant with light. Wondrously, this light seemed to be diffused like the midday sun all round the priest. In the process of beatification of the holy Franciscan Observant, Blessed Thomas of Cori, witnesses stated that on a dark morning the whole church had been lit up by the radiance that glowed in his face. And in what is apparently the earliest account of Blessed Giles of Assisi (d.1262), we are told that on one occasion in the night: 'so great a light shone round him that the light of the moon was wholly eclipsed thereby.'

Other accounts tell how the house of Blessed Aleidis of Scarbeke seemed to be on fire when she was praying within, the brightness coming from her radiant countenance; and how the cell of St Louis Bertran 'appeared as if the whole room was illuminated with the most powerful lamps.' The 15th-century German ecclesiastic Thomas à Kempis says of St Lydwina:

a state of ecstasy. In everyday speech, we talk of faces shining with happiness; and it could well be that this shining is sometimes more than mere metaphor.

In *Exodus 34,* for example, we read that when Moses came down from Mount Sinai with the two tablets containing God's commandments, 'the skin of his face shone.' This shining frightened everyone, so Moses put a veil over his face until he had finished speaking with his people. Similar glowings are described in *The Bible* with regard to St Paul's vision at the time of his conversion, and in the transfiguration of Christ, when his clothes became so shining that no 'fuller' or bleacher of cloth could equal its whiteness.

Nandor Fodor (1895-1964), the Hungarian writer on parapsychology, tells us that medieval saints and

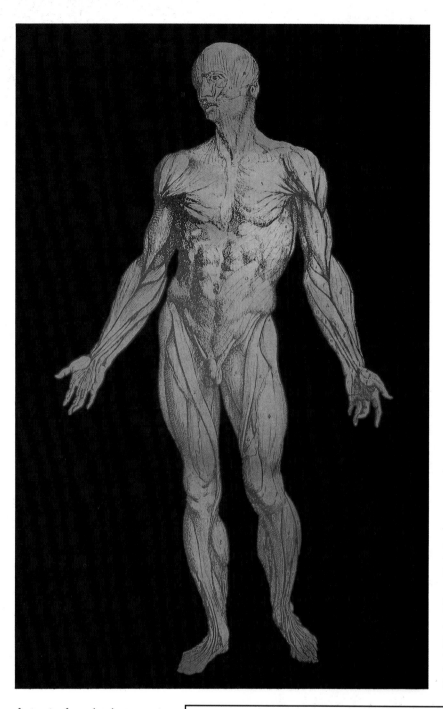

'And although she always lay in darkness, and material light was unbearable to her eyes, nevertheless the divine light was very agreeable to her, whereby her cell was often so wondrously flooded by night that, to the beholders, the cell itself appeared full of material lamps or fires. Nor is it strange if she overflowed even in the body with divine brightness. '

SAINTLY LUMINESCENCE

Father Herbert Thurston, in his highly regarded book, *The Physical Phenomena of Mysticism,* wrote of these records of saintly luminescence:

'Although a great number of these rest upon quite insufficient testimony, there are others which cannot lightly be set aside... There can, therefore, be no adequate reason for refusing credence to the report of similar phenomena when they are recorded of those whose eminent holiness and marvellous gifts of grace are universally recognised.'

Father Thurston cites two striking cases from the 17th century concerning the Blessed Bernardino Realini and Father Francisco Suárez.

The process leading to the beatification of Father Bernardino, who died in Lecce in Italy in 1616, was begun in Naples in 1621. Among the witnesses examined was Tobias da Ponte, a gentleman of rank and good standing. He testified that, in about 1608, he had gone to consult the Father. Before entering the room, he noticed a powerful glow that streamed around the door, which was slightly ajar, and through chinks in the boards. Wondering what could have prompted the Father to light a fire at midday in April, he pushed the door a little further open. There, he saw the Father kneeling, rapt in ecstasy and elevated about 2 feet (more than half-a-metre) above the floor. Da Ponte was so dazed by the spectacle that he sat down for a while, and then returned home without even making himself known to the priest.

Other people also bore witness to the extraordinary radiance of Father Bernardino's countenance. They had not seen him levitate, but some declared that they had seen sparks coming from all over his body, and others asserted that the dazzling glow from his face on one or two occasions was such that they could not properly distinguish his features, but had to turn their eyes away.

Accounts of people who appear to glow, represented by the figure, above, often ascribe the phenomenon to their holiness or a higher spiritual nature. Indeed, in much religious art, the divine person is very often shown surrounded by a visible aura – for example, a halo around the head – that is taken to symbolise his or her sanctity.

CASEBOOK

A COLOURFUL TALENT

The famous American psychic and healer, Edgar Cayce (1877-1945), asserted that, right from a very early age, he had always seen colours in association with people. Indeed, he claimed always to see reds, greens or blues pouring from the heads and shoulders of those he met. As he put it: 'For me, the aura is the weather-vane of the soul. It shows me the way the winds of destiny are blowing.'

It is, however, a talent that he believed could be developed by everyone. He was even convinced that the majority of us do see one another's aura but simply do not realise it. By taking note of the colours that people look best in and that they choose for their homes, Cayce held that we can begin to recognise the aura and the way in which it may change according to state of mind.

'All of you know what colours are helpful to your friends and bring out the best in them,' he wrote. 'They are the colours that beat with the same vibration as the aura, and thus strengthen and heighten it.' Thus, it seems, although the holy may 'glow' most of all, we are all surrounded by a degree of luminescence.

Mohammed, left, appears fully encircled by flames in this 16th-century painting from Turkey; Quetzalcoatl, below, the Aztec god, in his guise as the morning star is surrounded by fire on an ancient stele from Mexico; whilst the great Buddhist teacher Padmasambhava, below right, is haloed in an 18th-century painting from Tibet. Finally, the four kings of hell, bottom, on a Chinese hanging scroll, have crowned heads encircled by light.

Father Francisco Suárez, the subject of Father Thurston's second example, was a Spanish theologian who, from 1597 to 1617, taught at the Jesuit College at Coimbra in Portugal. One day at about 2 p.m., an elderly lay-brother, Jerome da Silva, came to tell the Father of the arrival of a visitor. A stick placed across the door indicated that the Father did not wish to be disturbed, but the lay-brother had received instructions to inform the Father at once, so he went in. He found the outer room in darkness, shuttered against the afternoon heat. Suárez's biographer, Father de Scorraille, records da Silva's account of the incident:

'I called the Father but he made no answer. As the curtain which shut off his working room was drawn, I saw, through the space between the jambs of the door and the curtain, a very great brightness. I pushed aside the curtain and entered the inner apartment. Then I noticed that the blinding light was coming from the crucifix, so intense that it was like the reflection of the sun from glass windows, and I felt that I could not have remained looking at it without being completely dazzled. This light streamed from the crucifix upon the face and breast of Father Suárez, and in the brightness I saw him in a kneeling position in front of the crucifix, his head uncovered, his hands joined, and his body in the air

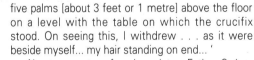

five palms [about 3 feet or 1 metre] above the floor on a level with the table on which the crucifix stood. On seeing this, I withdrew . . . as it were beside myself... my hair standing on end... '

About a quarter of an hour later, Father Suárez came out and was surprised to see Brother da Silva waiting. The account continues: 'When the Father heard that I had entered the inner room, he seized me by the arm . . . then, clasping his hands and with his eyes full of tears, he implored me to say nothing of what I had seen . . . as long as he lived.'

Father Suárez and da Silva shared the same confessor, who suggested that da Silva should write his account and seal it with the endorsement that it should not be opened and read until after the death of Father Suárez. That, apparently was done. The account provides us with a particularly compelling story of human luminescence – in this case, the glow of holiness.

PICTURES
FROM BEYOND
THE GRAVE

DOES ARTISTIC GENIUS DIE WITH THE ARTIST – OR COULD IT POSSIBLY SURVIVE, TO FIND EXPRESSION THROUGH THE HANDS OF LIVING PSYCHICS?

Pablo Picasso, who died in April 1973, produced several drawings in both pen-and-ink and colour, three months afterwards – through British psychic Matthew Manning. While concentrating, Manning found his hand being controlled with an assertive force, apparently by the spirit of the great master. He had specifically asked Picasso to produce a drawing for him.

Psychic art presents many of the same questions to the psychical researcher that are posed by the prize-winning psychic literature of Patience Worth or Beethoven's 1980 symphony. Is the painting, poetry or music, believed by many to be evidence of the artist's survival beyond the grave, merely an exhibition of the medium's own repressed creativity, finally finding expression? Or is it really as simple as the psychics would have us

The style of the work above left is unmistakably Aubrey Beardsley's, but the pen-and-ink drawing was actually produced through the hands of English psychic Matthew Manning.

The posthumous Picasso, above, was also painted by Matthew Manning, who remarked on the 'energy and impatience' of the artist. Picasso is one of the few artists who 'chose' to use colour when working through Manning.

A Manning-Monet is shown, above right. The style certainly seems to be consistent with that of the great French impressionist.

The drawing, right, of a hanged man, is by Leonardo da Vinci. Manning once found himself drawing something very similar but suddenly felt physically ill and wanted to stop the drawing.

believe – that the world's great musicians, writers and artists are 'proving' their continued existence by carrying on their arts through selected 'sensitives'?

Some examples of psychic art are highly impressive, both in their own right and, more significantly, as examples of the styles of the great painters. Some collections of psychic art are also impressive in their diversity of style and sheer quantity.

It was Matthew Manning's enormous collection of sketches and paintings, seemingly produced psychically by him as a teenager in the early 1970s, that utterly convinced his publisher that he was a very special young man, particularly as Manning claims to have no ability at all to draw.

CONTACT WITH THE DEAD

Manning's intelligent, articulate and objective approach to all the strange phenomena in his life makes fascinating reading. In his first book, *The Link*, he discusses his method of 'contacting' dead artists. He simply sat quietly with a pad and pen in hand and concentrated on the artist. As he himself put it: 'I empty my mind as completely as possible and in that state I think of the person I am trying to contact – sending all my energy out to this person who then writes or draws through my hand'. Almost immediately, the pen would begin to move, usually starting in the centre of the page and finally filling it with what seemed like a well-planned work of art. Almost always, the result was recognisably in the style of the artist on whom he had been concentrating: sometimes it was even signed. Occasionally, however, although bearing a strong resemblance to the style of the artist he had wanted to 'reach', the pictures were not signed. In these instances, it seemed to Manning that some other discarnate artist, perhaps even a pupil of the greater one, had intervened.

The communicators also showed very distinct personalities. 'No other communicator tires me out

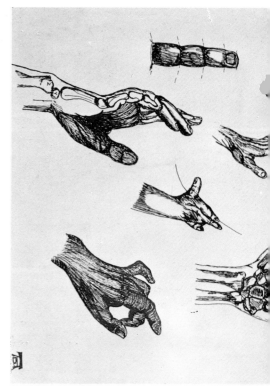

mistakes made and covered over. It took between one and two hours to produce a finished work, whereas most living artists would perhaps take days to produce a painting of similar size and complexity – and then not necessarily of the same high quality. More time would also have been spent in planning and sketching.

But one psychic artist has produced 'new' old masters at the rate of 21 in 75 minutes. In March 1978, the Brazilian Luiz Gasparetto appeared on BBC's *Nationwide* and was seen by millions to go into a trance and produce 21 pictures – sometimes

as much as Picasso does,' Manning has said. 'After only a few minutes, the time it takes him to do one drawing, I feel worn out and cannot continue for at least 24 hours...'

Pablo Picasso was also one of the few communicators who was not confused about using colour: indeed, he directed Matthew Mannings's hand to pick out certain felt-tipped pens from a box of mixed colours. (Most of Manning's other discarnate artists used pen-and-ink.)

DIVERSITY OF STYLE

Among the signed works in his collection are drawings recognisably in the styles of Arthur Rackham, Paul Klee, Leonardo da Vinci, Albrecht Dürer, Aubrey Beardsley, Beatrix Potter, Pablo Picasso, Keble Martin and the Elizabethan miniaturist, Isaac Oliver.

Sometimes a finished picture would be very similar to a famous work by a particular artist, but usually these similarities had to be pointed out to him. A virtual reproduction of Beardsley's famous *Salome*, for example, took place under his very eyes as he concentrated on Beardsley.

The 'new' work usually came at an incredible speed. There was no preliminary sketching, nor – except in the case of Aubrey Beardsley – were any

Four centuries after his death, Isaac Oliver – the Elizabethan miniaturist – executed and signed such detailed – and typical – work as the picture above, via Matthew Manning.

Albrecht Dürer (1471-1528), inventor of engraving and true son of the Renaissance, was another of Matthew Manning's alleged communicators. The rhinoceros, above right, and the study of human hands, right – 'transmitted through' Matthew Manning – are characteristic of Dürer's minute observation and the scope of his interests.

The crayon drawing by Brazilian trance artist Luiz Antonio Gasparetto, right, is in the style of Henri de Toulouse-Lautrec (1864-1901). Whereas most of Gasparetto's paintings take only a few minutes to complete, this one took several hours. The drawing was made in 1978 while the medium was living in London, studying English.

Sometimes painted with both hands simultaneously, sometimes with his toes, and almost always within a few minutes, Luiz Gasparetto's trance-paintings bear striking resemblances to the works of famous, dead artists. Often the 'spirit' paintings are signed, such as the typical Van Gogh, right – signed 'Vincent' – and the slightly unusual Picasso, far right. Others do not need a full signature: the style is sufficient. Who else could have painted the closely-observed portrait, below, but Toulouse-Lautrec, or Gasparetto?

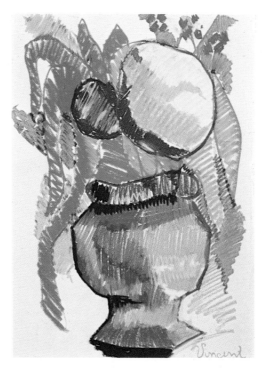

working with both hands simultaneously on two separate pictures, producing perfect paintings, even though he executed them upside down – and all so fast that many viewers believed the BBC had accelerated the film. The results were apparently 'new' Renoirs, Cézannes and Picassos.

Gasparetto found working under the harsh studio lights very trying, because he normally paints – in a trance – in the dark or, at most, in a very weak light. A psychologist by profession, he views what he produces with some objectivity. But, although familiar with others who write or paint by psychic means, he says: 'I've never seen anyone else who can draw with both hands in the dark – in 30 different styles.' In a state of normal consciousness, he even says that, like Manning, he cannot paint at all.

This Brazilian says he sees, senses and talks to all the great artists who 'come through'. Interestingly, particularly in view of Matthew Manning's experience, Gasparetto has revealed: 'Picasso sometimes used to be violent. If anyone whispered, he would throw the paper away.'

Gasparetto travels extensively with journalist and fellow spiritist Elsie Dubugras, giving demonstrations of psychic painting. After each session, the paintings are then auctioned and the proceeds go to charity.

Although Gasparetto is still producing vast numbers of psychic paintings, Matthew Manning has done little automatic art or writing since adolescence. At first, he did it because he found it quelled the poltergeist activity that seemed always to surround him; but now it appears that the power, whatever it is, has been harnessed for the healing with which he has become involved.

Researchers and sceptics alike have come up with theories of repressed creativity, or even a secondary personality, to account for the strange phenomenon of psychic art. Perhaps we will never know how, or why, it happens; but out of all the vast array of paranormal phenomena, this threatens no one – and often produces works of great beauty.

FROM RUSSIA WITH PSI

RESEARCH AND EXPERIMENT
IN PARAPSYCHOLOGY IS
KNOWN TO HAVE THRIVED
BEHIND THE IRON CURTAIN,
ATTRACTING THE INTEREST
OF SECURITY AND MILITARY
OFFICIALS WORLDWIDE

In 1957, only three articles appeared on the subject of parapsychology in the entire Soviet press, and all were hostile. Yet ten years later, the total had risen to 152, and less than 10 per cent were negative or even critical. Psychic matters had suddenly become respectable; and, as a steady stream of western journalists soon discovered, there was plenty to write about. All over the Soviet Union, it seemed, talented subjects were demonstrating paranormal abilities to scientists who, in turn, were eager to share their new discoveries with western colleagues. The Soviets were, in fact, just as interested as anybody else in telepathy, psychokinesis, UFOs, paranormal healing, and the rest of the *psi* spectrum.

Following the death of the Russian scientist and parapsychologist Leonid Vasiliev in 1966, a new generation of Soviet researchers, many directly inspired by his pioneering research into telepathy, was ready to carry on and expand his work. The young physicist, Viktor Adamenko, for example, had

Until the breakup of the USSR in 1991, Soviet power was usually represented by its missiles, bottom. Some people, however, believed a greater threat lay in its research into telepathy and other forms of mind control.

Dr Genady Sergeyev, a neurophysiologist, is seen above with his invention – a 'bioenergy measuring device'.

started to study the psychokinetic talent of his wife, Alla Vinogradova. Dr G.A. Sergeyev, a mathematician and neurophysiologist, was deeply involved in research into Man's interactions – both normal and paranormal – with his environment. Biochemist Yuri Kamensky had shown himself to be an unusually successful transmitter of images and targets, and his long-distance telepathy experiments with actor Karl Nikolayev fully supported earlier work by Vasiliev. At the Kazakh State University in Alma-Ata, biophysicist Dr V. M. Inyushin was evolving his theory of 'bioplasma' and developing the high-frequency photographic technique popularised by Semyon and Valentina Kirlian.

STAR PERFORMERS

These scientists had many star performers with whom to work. Nina Kulagina, for instance, was willing to demonstrate her psychokinetic abilities to order, whether to scientists in laboratories or to western visitors in hotel rooms. Rosa Kuleshova repeatedly proved her ability to read with her fingertips. Boris Yermolayev satisfied astonished observers, including the eminent psychologist Dr Venyami Pushkin, that he could levitate objects and even people. The young Azerbaijani Tofik Dadashev also set out to carry on the stage tradition set by world-famous 'mentalist' Wolf Messing, and brought publicly demonstrated telepathy into almost every city in the Soviet Union.

Behind all this excitement, scientists led by Dr Ippolit Kogan, head of the newly-formed Bioinformation Section of a Moscow technical institute, were hard at work on theoretical aspects of *psi*. And although parapsychology had never been

Dr Viktor Inyushin, a biophysicist at Kazakh State University, bottom left, undertook research into Kirlian photography, officially approved by the state.

Soviet actor Karl Nikolayev, below right, was the subject of many successful experiments into long-distance telepathy.

Soviet parapsychologist Viktor Adamenko, above, holds a small electric light bulb that lit up when placed beside an object that had been moved psychokinetically by his wife, Alla Vinogradova. In another display of her remarkable abilities, Vinogradova, right, shifts a metal cigar tube by passing her hand over it.

Petrich, spend the night in the state hotel built especially for Dimitrova's clients and sleep with a sugar lump under his pillow. The next day, he would visit Dimitrova and, when he reached the head of the queue, she would take the sugar lump from him, press it to her forehead, and immediately reel off a flood of information about his past, present and future. Bulgaria also boasted another world first: its official parapsychology institute in the centre of Sofia, headed by Georgi Lozanov, a medical doctor who, like thousands of other Bulgarians, had received accurate personal information from Dimitrova. He was later to become famous for his method of rapid learning through a method termed 'suggestology'.

EAST-WEST DIALOGUE

During the 1960s, Eastern Europe was indeed a centre of parapsychology. But this was not to last. In 1968, Eduard Naumov organised an international conference in Moscow, which was attended by nine westerners, including journalists Lynn Schroeder and Sheila Ostrander from the USA. Hardly had the meeting begun when the Russian newspaper *Pravda* came out with a savage attack on parapsychology in general, and medium Nina Kulagina in particular. Delegates were dismissed from the House of Friendship, and word went round that the East-West dialogue between parapsychologists was over.

Matters were made even worse when Schroeder and Ostrander published *Psychic Discoveries Behind The Iron Curtain* in 1970. This popular book contained an enormous amount of information on developments in Eastern Europe and the USSR, previously unknown to westerners, and

recognised as a scientific discipline in its own right, a young biologist, Eduard Naumov, was devoting himself to it full-time, determined to increase and improve East-West relations by means of his chosen field of research.

Elsewhere in Eastern Europe, the psychic scene looked equally promising, especially in Czechoslovakia, where Dr Milan Ryzl was showing that paranormal skills could be aroused through intensive training and use of hypnosis. Working over a three-year period with a single subject, Pavel Stepanek, he achieved positive results, nine times out of ten, in card-guessing experiments, several of which were witnessed by western visitors. He had, he claimed, published details of the first demonstration of repeatable telepathy under laboratory conditions. 'The subject,' he announced, 'evidently and repeatedly manifested the faculty of extra-sensory perception.'

Also in Czechoslovakia, engineer-inventor Robert Pavlita had begun to arouse considerable interest with his 'psychotronic generators' – small metal objects with which, he claimed, he was able to store 'biological energy'.

Meanwhile, Bulgaria had become the first country in the world to boast a state-supported psychic, a blind woman named Vanga Dimitrova from the small southern town of Petrich, near the Greek border. Any visitor could walk into the Sofia office of Balkantourist, the state travel agency, and book a sitting with her. The subject would then drive to

led to a considerable increase of interest in them. It also made it clear that the Soviets were way ahead of the field in most areas of research into the paranormal. But Soviet authorities did not like the book at all. It was, they said, 'overflowing with factual errors and undisguised anti-Soviet thrusts'; and they reacted violently to the suggestion that parapsychology was linked to defence, psychological warfare or espionage.

Reliable observers consider, however, that what really angered the authorities was the indiscretion of Naumov, who had revealed a couple of state secrets: one, that the Soviet military had carried out experiments in animal telepathy between a submarine and the shore; the other, that a method had been devised to intercept telepathy between

humans. Both these reports, if true, could have considerable military significance: conventional communication with a submerged submarine can be extremely difficult; and if telepathy were to become a weapon of war, a means of intercepting it would be of the greatest value.

TRUMPED-UP CHARGE

Although Naumov managed to organise another highly successful international meeting in 1972, he was in serious trouble the following year – allegedly for a financial misdemeanour. He was arrested and sentenced to two years' forced labour in March 1974. Perhaps as a result of vigorous international protest, he was released a year later. However, he was not allowed to resume work and disappeared altogether from the parapsychological scene.

Then, in October 1973, the Soviet press published an article that seemed, at last, to define the official attitude towards parapsychology. It also went some way towards explaining the USSR's apparently erratic international relations. The message was clear. *Psi* phenomena did indeed exist – some of them, anyway – and should be researched, but not by amateurs or 'militant individuals' (a clear reference to Naumov), but by the Soviet Academy of Sciences instead.

Normal international relations were, to all appearances, resumed when, largely on the initiatives of two psychologists – Dr Stanley Krippner (USA) and Dr Zdenek Rejdak (Czechoslovakia) – the first International Conference on Psychotronic Research was held in Prague in 1973: (*Psychotronics* is the Czech term for parapsychology). More than 400 delegates from 21 countries attended, including a group from the Soviet Academy of Sciences, and several Soviet and Eastern European scientists made important contributions. 'There is no doubt that we are experiencing the birth of a unique science,' said Krippner of the study of psychotronics, 'one which requires a combination of the physical and behavioural sciences with a new, holistic viewpoint on the organisation of life systems.'

A solid bridge had at last, it seemed, been built. Several western researchers visited the Eastern bloc countries, and formed close friendships with their counterparts there. Further parapsychological congresses were held at two-yearly intervals; and although there was no Soviet presence in Monaco in 1975 or in Tokyo in 1977, a team of Moscow medical researchers attended the 1979 gathering in Brazil, where Dr Rejdak made a firm plea for placing psychotronic research above politics.

ANALYSING REACTIONS

One might have thought that Schroeder and Ostrander had closed the door for other western writers; but in 1975, two American reporters from the sensationalist weekly *National Enquirer* were given free access to several Soviet research centres, including some that were off limits even to Soviet journalists. Reporters Henry Gris and William Dick were as surprised as anybody else at the privilege they had been granted; but one Soviet scientist speculated that his country's authorities were just as curious about western advances in

parapsychology as westerners were about theirs. They wanted to find out how advanced the West really was, he thought, by studying reactions to what Gris and Dick reported.

Yet, even as Gris and Dick were preparing a book on their findings, a bizarre incident took place in 1977 that seemed to put the clock back to the chilliest period of the cold war of the 1950s. On 11 June, the *Los Angeles Times* correspondent in Moscow, Robert C. Toth, was telephoned by a man named Petukhov, who asked to meet him in the street at once. Toth did so, and was handed a document; but before he had time even to glance at it, both men were surrounded by plainclothes police and driven off for lengthy interrogation.

Then, a man claiming to be a senior member of the Academy of Sciences, promptly appeared, read the document, and announced that it contained an account of recent Soviet discoveries on the physical basis of *psi* phenomena – something they had sought in vain for half a century – and that it was a state secret. After 13 hours of interrogation by the KGB, Toth was released, and allowed to leave the country.

This incident baffled western observers as much as it did Toth himself, who had never shown any interest in parapsychology. It was thought at the

authorities in possible uses of it. Practical application had always been a characteristic of all Soviet research; and once it became possible to make practical use of *psi*, Dr Ryzl concluded, 'there is no doubt that the Soviet Union will do so'.

Western researchers have repeatedly been urged by their Eastern counterparts to ensure that psychic forces are used for peace and for the benefit of humanity. 'There is something about the way they say this,' one western parapsychologist has said, 'that makes it clear to me that some people have other ideas.'

// FROM CIA AGENTS STATIONED BEHIND THE IRON CURTAIN CAME REPORTS THAT THE RUSSIANS WERE ABLE TO INFLUENCE TELEPATHICALLY THE BEHAVIOUR OF PEOPLE, ALTER THEIR EMOTIONS OR HEALTH, AND EVEN KILL AT LONG DISTANCE BY USING ONLY PSYCHIC POWER. //

GRIS AND DICK, THE NEW SOVIET PSYCHIC DISCOVERIES

A selection of the various types of psychotronic generator, invented by Robert Pavlita, above, are displayed top. They could, he claimed, store biological energy.

time that he was merely being warned off any involvement with dissidents, but this is unlikely in view of the fact that he had finished his tour and was due to leave anyway. A more probable explanation is that the whole episode was set up by the authorities, and was a clumsy bluff. The Soviets had not solved the *psi* mystery, but they wanted the West to think they had, and hoped that Toth would report something to this effect to his newspaper.

TERRIFYING WARFARE

There was another more alarming theory, too. In 1973, the Soviet leader Leonid Brezhnev had made an enigmatic reference in a speech to a form of warfare 'more terrifying' than even nuclear weaponry, and the need for the USA to agree to a ban on it. He gave the impression that he knew the American leaders would know what he meant. Was this perhaps a veiled reference to biochemical (germ) warfare? Or had the Toth affair been a gentle reminder to the West that the Soviets were now in a position to wage psychic warfare?

After visiting the USSR, shortly before he went to live in the United States, Milan Ryzl reported on a paradoxical state of affairs there. Parapsychology, he said, was poorly funded; yet there were signs of considerable interest from security and military

In the group portrait, above left, American journalists Lynn Schroeder, left, and Sheila Ostrander, right, are seen with Soviet parapsychologist Eduard Naumov in Moscow in 1968, during the First International Conference on Parapsychology. Ostrander and Schroeder published their findings in Psychic Discoveries Behind The Iron Curtain in 1970, a book swiftly denounced by Soviet authorities.

Vanga Dimitrova, Bulgaria's famous blind prophetess, right, was the world's first known state-financed psychic. Sittings with her could be booked through the Bulgarian state travel agency.

CAN THE MIND SOMEHOW
TRAVEL MANY MILES,
TOUR A TARGET LOCATION
AND REPORT BACK WITH
AN ACCURATE DESCRIPTION?
THERE ARE MANY
CONTROVERSIAL CLAIMS
MADE FOR THE BIZARRE
PHENOMENON OF
REMOTE VIEWING

When Russell Targ and Harold Puthoff published *Mind-reach* in 1977, they were not modest about its claims: they had, they asserted, made the final breakthrough and established scientifically that the phenomenon known as remote viewing was fact. What was more, they considered it to be 'probably a latent and widely distributed perceptual ability.'

Remote viewing – a form of ESP – was not a new subject for discussion and experiment. Papers covering aspects of the phenomenon had appeared in the early 1970s in the British science journal *Nature*, as well as in other highly respected publications. Although controversial, it was believed to be a subject to be taken seriously, Targ and Puthoff's work in this field especially so, for they were both

The pioneering work into remote viewing of Russell Targ, bottom left, and Harold Puthoff, right, respected physicists of California's Stanford Research Institute, was savagely attacked by scientists and psychical researchers alike.

established physicists on the academic staff of California's Stanford Research Institute (SRI).

Their standing as reputable scientists and the confident way they presented their case made it impossible to ignore their claims. Nevertheless, their research was subjected to intense scrutiny – and the reaction they received was little short of savage.

Targ and Puthoff were accused of everything – from deliberately misreading the results and prompting the subjects to unscientific methodology. Even so, they invited other scientists to try to reproduce their results. But to many psychical researchers, it seemed that remote viewing, like so many other similar 'breakthroughs', was a kind of mirage. Was it possible that the researchers trying to reproduce the results of Targ and Puthoff's work had missed some element in the experiments? Or was it that the two physicists had, in their enthusiasm, pushed their conclusions too far?

Targ and Puthoff began their experiments with a series of remarkable successes, using as subjects a New York artist and psychic, Ingo Swann, and a retired police commissioner, Pat Price. Both showed remarkable aptitude for remote viewing; in some cases, they even named the target location instead of merely describing it. Sometimes, they were given only map co-ordinates and asked to describe in detail what they 'saw'.

These and other successes inspired Targ and Puthoff to mount more tightly controlled experiments in order to validate beyond doubt the phenomenon of remote viewing.

Altogether, there were nine experiments using Pat Price, which were duly written up and published in *Nature* in October 1974. In these papers, a high

REMOTE VIEWING

Startlingly accurate though much of this was, many of Price's transcripts also included much that was incorrect. The researchers began to see a pattern in his remote viewing, noting 'the occurrence of essentially correct descriptions of basic elements and patterns, coupled with incomplete or erroneous analysis of function, was to be a continuing thread throughout the remote viewing work.' In other words, he was often muddled or wrong.

The scientists also noted that Price drew target locations or objects as mirror images, which proved – to them – that the right hemisphere of the brain was somehow involved in the process, for the right side of the brain is believed to control holistic, pattern-making and intuitive thinking.

Impressive as Price's results were to those who worked closely with him, the real test came when the transcripts and drawings were compared with the target areas by an independent judge who visited the nine sites and then rated the accuracy of the descriptions on a scale of one to nine. He had been

proportion of the transcript description is very specific – some might have thought suspiciously so. Perhaps it was for this very reason that the series provoked a most hostile reaction.

Nine target locations in the Stanford area were chosen. Before the experiment began, these were noted down, and each was sealed in an envelope before being locked away in a safe. Pat Price and an experimenter – usually Russell Targ – stationed themselves in a room about 30 minutes before remote viewing was due to begin. Meanwhile, Harold Puthoff, together with at least one other member of the target team, selected an envelope at random from the safe, opened it, and set off for the specified location. Neither Price nor Targ had any communication with the rest of the team from the beginning of the test.

A PERFECT DESCRIPTION

The first site was a well-known landmark on the Stanford campus, the Hoover Tower. Not only did Price immediately describe a tower-like structure, but actually specified it as the 'Hoover Tower'.

This seemed almost too good to be true. The protocol of the experiments was then tightened to prevent security leaks. The divisional director, whose function it was to open the target envelope, now drove the team to the site before revealing its identity to them. The first time they did this, the target was Redwood City Marina, south of San Francisco. Price's first taped words were: 'What I'm looking at is a little boat jetty or... dock along the bay.'

Another bull's eye description was given for the seventh target on the list – an arts and crafts plaza with shops, flowers, ceramic ornaments, fountains, paths and vine-hung arbors. In the report, Price's unedited transcript is quoted verbatim. Targ and Puthoff claimed his 'description is accurate in almost every detail'.

Indeed, Price's 'viewing' contained much that was specifically relevant to the arts and crafts plaza. He said, for example: 'I'm looking at something that looks like an arbor... Seems to be cool, shaded. Doesn't seem to me that they're [i.e. the target team] out in the direct sunlight... there's lots of trees, in an arbor area.'

The machine, top, was devised by Targ and Puthoff. The subject has to indicate which image is going to flash on a screen seconds before it appears. This apparatus was also used in psi testing by Professor Hans Bender and Elmar Gruber of the Freiburg Institute in Germany.

presented with Price's unlabelled narratives in a random order, so he had no hint as to which site Price had been referring – except from the scripts themselves. Having carried out this evaluation, the judge awarded him seven direct hits out of nine, a strikingly significant result.

Further back-up was provided when a separate group of SRI scientists, so far unassociated with the Targ/Puthoff programme, was asked to match the scripts against the targets. The same procedure as before was followed: unlabelled, randomly ordered transcripts were distributed to a team of five, who then visited the sites independently.

Chance alone would have provided five correct matches overall; but in this test, the correct correlation was much higher. Individually, the investigation team scored them seven, six, five, three and three.

But the most fascinating aspect of Price's involvement was that he, although obviously a successful

Hella Hammid's drawing of the target that she described as 'some kind of diagonal trough up in the air' is seen above. Compare it with the target – a pedestrian overpass; the perspective is particularly accurate.

Another sketch of a target, as 'seen' by one of the SRI subjects, is shown above left, with a photograph of the actual location – San Andres airport in Colombia, South America. It would appear to be a remarkable 'hit'.

'viewer', did not claim to possess any special gift for it: he merely said that he was willing to give the experiments a try. If it were true that he had no special 'talent' and yet was so strikingly successful, the researchers wondered if *anyone* could do it.

The team now found a suitable guinea-pig for the next stage in the series in Hella Hammid, a professional photographer. Another nine experiment series was mounted, along similar lines to that using Price. The only difference was that Hammid's remote viewing time was cut from 30 to 15 minutes.

DRAWING CONCLUSIONS

Hammid preferred to make drawings of her mental impressions, rather than describe them verbally, as Price had done. Some of these 'doodles' were remarkably accurate.

Again, an independent judge was brought in to repeat the matching process, and the results were just as impressive: five direct hits and four second ranks. The odds against this were given as 500,000:1.

Following up this success, Targ and Puthoff ran a further four series of tests, involving seven other subjects. All but one test proved to be statistically significant.

These results should, indeed, as *Mind-reach* claimed, have proved beyond a shadow of doubt that remote viewing is fact. However, the experiments and their results were not always straightforward, nor easy to evaluate. For example, when the late Dr Kit Pedler was making his series *Mind Over Matter* for British television, and visited Stanford to take part in an experiment himself, certain problems emerged.

Hella Hammid acted as subject, while Dr Pedler and Dr Beverley Rubik, a biologist who had joined up with the team for the experiment, drove off to one of the six randomly selected sites in the vicinity. Television viewers saw Pedler and Rubik wandering round a rocky incline, while Hammid – locked in a hotel room – was being filmed, speaking and drawing her impressions of what they were seeing.

After a specified period, Pedler and Rubik returned to the hotel and compared notes with Hammid. Then Hammid was driven to each of the six sites with the task of identifying the target with only her previously recorded impressions as guides. As it happened, she was convinced she had not 'seen' the target – but, instead, identified one of the other sites on the list, Codornices Park, as the place she had 'seen'.

Dr Pedler found the very nature of this 'miss' intriguing. Though some may think his reasoning merely desperate rationalization in an embarrassing situation, he pointed out that there is a well-known, if little understood, factor called the 'displacement effect'. This is an extremely mysterious process, found also in other telepathic experiments, which operates when the subject homes in not on the target itself but on one of the others in the target pool. The phenomenon frequently goes unremarked because researchers are concerned solely with totalling up direct hits. To many, including Dr Pedler, this aspect of telepathic experiment was potentially just as exciting as getting direct hits.

But in the case of the Puthoff/Targ experiments, more mundane objections were also raised. On only

very few occasions was the received image unambiguously clear. There may, indeed, be a number of correct correspondences, but in most cases there is an abundance of over-generalized description: trees. roads, flowers, hills and so on – easily guessed components of many likely target sites. Sifting out the relevant from the 'padding', and agreeing on the precise significance of each phrase in the transcript, is clearly not quite as easy as the experimenters stated.

Yet, despite these quibbles, Targ and Puthoff did seem to present a strikingly positive case for remote viewing. So why did the critics attack them so fiercely?

Two of the sceptics were David Marks and Richard Kamman, both psychologists at New Zealand's Otago University. Their students, reading of Puthoff and Targ's conclusions, had begun to bombard them with questions about remote viewing and parapsychology in general. The Stanford Research Institute (SRI) had suddenly become the centre of attention.

Neither Marks nor Kamman had, until that point in the late 1970s, any special interest in ESP, and they admitted their relative ignorance about parapsychology. But the pressure from their students was so intense that they realised they would have to give it attention. They were interested in the SRI experiments particularly, because Targ and Puthoff had claimed that almost anyone, psychically gifted or not, could be successful in remote viewing tests. It was also claimed that the results of the experiments were easy to reproduce.

So, between 1976 and 1978, Marks and Kamman ran 35 trials that were similar to the SRI sessions. They used five subjects: a graduate psychologist, a hypnotist, a housewife, an arts student and a medical undergraduate. All of them expressed the belief that they had some psychic ability.

Marks and Kamman followed the SRI routines as faithfully as possible. The target team was given 20 minutes to reach its specified destination, then the subject – back at the laboratory – noted down any feelings or impressions about the unknown target for 15 minutes. The team returned, collected the subject, and all then went to the target site to check the subject's transcript against the location. Marks and Kamman were pleased to find encouraging correspondences at the early stages of their project. One of their subjects was so confident that he said: 'If the judges can't match my descriptions accurately, there will be something wrong with them.'

Unfortunately, this confidence was misplaced – the independent judges, brought in to try to match transcripts with actual target locations, failed to do so in every case that they were asked to consider.

WILLING SUCCESS

Up to this stage, everyone at Otago had felt very positive about the outcome of the experiments; so what had gone wrong? Marks and Kamman decided to accompany one subject and the target group on one of their joint trips to the target location after the actual remote viewing had taken place. This was to reveal serious flaws in the nature of the experiment – and, by implication, the experiments of Puthoff and Targ, whose methodology they had followed so carefully. The New Zealanders labelled the problem 'subjective validation': put simply, this means that if you want an experiment to work, it will – because you will tend to select the results you were seeking and reject the rest. Since all the subjects had been strongly motivated to succeed, they had tended to grasp at correspondences – between their impressions and the target – that, according to the judges, simply did not exist.

For their part, the judges had tried hard to match transcripts against targets, and they felt they had come up with the best matches possible. Unfortunately, these were not the same details seized upon as 'proof' by the experimental team.

The Otago team then asked the question: if we have had this difficulty, then how did Targ and Puthoff manage to achieve so many direct hits? They began to investigate the SRI findings in closer detail and came up with some provocative discoveries about the way the transcripts had been judged.

For example, they noticed that the SRI transcripts were unedited, including all manner of material in addition to the subject's actual narrative. Only some scripts were dated, and others – significantly – carried references to previous experiments. One of Pat Price's transcripts – the Redwood City Marina test – expressly mentioned the previous day's target: 'I've been trying to picture it in my mind and where you went yesterday on your nature walk... ' the transcript ran.

Marks and Kamman saw this as a potential cue to the judge, who was ostensibly trying to evaluate the material on its descriptive content alone. In effect, this apparently throwaway remark could have told the judge that, whatever the target was, it was not a nature walk, because that was the previous target. With such cues, the judge could have worked out the series of targets, consciously or subconsciously, and given higher scores as a result.

In an article written in 1927, Sir Oliver Lodge cited as evidence for 'telepathy at a distance' the case of the Misses Miles and Ramsden. They undertook a series of experiments in telepathy, which were similar to those carried out in the 1970s at SRI. Miss Miles photographed Henbury Church in Cheshire, above, while Miss Ramsden, in Scotland, drew her mental impressions of the image being transmitted, left. Miss Ramsden, however, felt dissatisfied, saying 'something is wanting, as it seemed bigger and more imposing'. The general shape is correct, but the lack of ivy and the slit windows suggest that she had somehow 'picked up' an early version of the church.

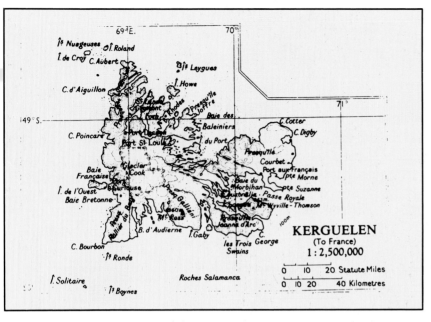

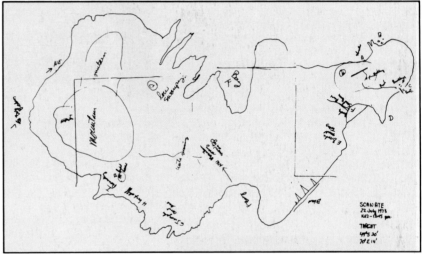

viewing session. Any extraneous matter showed not only bad, but suspicious, methodology.

With a little intelligent guesswork, and a little reading between the – added – lines, Marks correctly matched all five transcripts to the targets, 'solely on the basis of the cues contained in the transcripts, and no visits to target locations... prior to the successful matchings.'

Marks and Kamman therefore argued that the SRI judging could hardly be said to have been blind. Their conclusion, as published in *Nature*, says:

'Our investigation of the SRI remote viewing experiment with Pat Price forces the conclusion that the successful identification of target sites by judges is impossible unless multiple extraneous cues, which were available in the original unedited transcripts, are utilized. Investigators of remote viewing should take more care to ensure that such cues are not available. Furthermore, the listing of targets given to judges should be randomized and not presented in the same sequence as that which occurred in the experiments.'

What the SRI trials had not included, and what they badly needed, according to the Otago team, was an attempt at remote judging. Was it possible, they wondered, that the judges could come up with good matches armed only with the transcripts – that is, not visiting the target site at all?

The two psychologists acquired five of the Price scripts that had not been published from a consultant to the SRI project. These appeared to be covered in cues, such as references to 'yesterday's two targets', more specifically 'the second of the day', and Targ's encouraging comment on one transcript, 'nothing like having three successes behind you'. Other subtle cues included mention of the time of day of the experiment. In a rigidly controlled scientific experiment, there should have been nothing but the subject's impressions on the transcript, and only references to that particular remote

Project Scanate (scanning by coordinate) was one of the most controversial areas of SRI's remote viewing experiments. A map coordinate would be given to the team by telephone and the subject was asked to describe the location which would later be checked. According to Puthoff and Targ, psychic Ingo Swann, left, showed remarkable talent for this. The map co-ordinates for Kerguelen Island in the Indian Ocean, top, were given to Swann, who responded with an extremely accurate verbal description of the location. His version of the map, above, is however much less convincing, especially considering that Swann was also an artist and used to thinking in visual terms.

And what about the astonishingly successful SRI remote viewing tests using Ingo Swann and Hella Hammid? On balance, Marks and Kamman seriously doubted whether tighter controls had been involved in those. Their final, damning verdict, published in their book *The Psychology of the Psychic*, is that: 'It appears to us that the remote viewing effect is, at present, nothing more than a massive artifact of poor methodology and wishful thinking.'

But they did admit that they had been working with incomplete data and, of course, they had not been present during the SRI tests.

However, Professor Robert Morris, who reviewed *The Psychology of the Psychic* in the *Journal of the American Society for Psychical Research* (ASPR), investigated the New Zealanders' criticisms and, in turn, found much to criticize. They had, he asserted, jumped to as many conclusions as, in their opinion, had Puthoff and Targ. Marks and Kamman, said Morris, had overstepped the mark by juggling with incomplete or improperly understood data, reaching the wrong conclusions.

Sloppy methodology is one thing, but does it totally invalidate the basic premise that different people, in different places, can somehow 'see' with each other's eyes, telepathically?

THE PHENOMENAL FEATS OF MENTAL COMPUTATION ACHIEVED BY A FEW REMARKABLE PEOPLE ARE CERTAINLY FAR BEYOND NORMAL HUMAN CAPABILITY. WHO ARE THESE SUPERNOVA PERFORMERS?

HUMAN CALCU

In today's age of cheap pocket calculators, many of us are in danger of losing whatever arithmetical skill we may once have possessed. In former times, a shop assistant, confronted with six similar items at 25p each, would make an instant mental calculation that 25p x 6 = £1.50 and would punch that figure on the cash register. Nowadays, in the same situation, a shop assistant will probably use the cash register as a calculator. Whereas children once mastered multiplication tables as a basic skill, they now tend to use their trusty calculator to discover, say, what 4 x 9 equals.

Compared with previous generations, many of us could be said to be arithmetically illiterate. But in past centuries there have been human beings whose calculating ability so far outshone that of their contemporaries and predecessors that mathematicians, scientists and psychologists alike have been astounded. Appearing at random like meteors,

such 'lightning calculators' demonstrate that the human brain is capable of feats that remain largely unexplained.

Some of these lightning calculators have been exceptionally gifted in other spheres of human activity, too; others, in contrast, have exhibited a stupidity that threw their strange mathematical talent into bizarre relief. The only thing common to most of them is that they demonstrated their extraordinary gift in early childhood. With some, it lasted throughout their lives; with others, it departed after a few years. Like the infant musical prodigies, Chopin and Mozart, who both played brilliantly and composed at an early age, the mathematical prodigies seem to have been either self-taught or somehow simply endowed with their ability.

The Irish mathematician Sir William Hamilton (1805-1865) is a good example of someone with exceptional all-round ability. He began to learn Hebrew at the age of three; and by the time he was seven, a fellow of Trinity College, Dublin, said that he showed a greater knowledge of the language than many candidates for a fellowship. By the age of 13, he knew at least 13 languages. Of his early mathematical ability, a relative said: 'I remember him a little boy of six, when he would answer a difficult mathematical question, and run off gaily to his little cart'.

The German mathematician and scientist, Carl Friedrich Gauss (1777-1855), also demonstrated an exceptional early ability to carry out mathematical calculations in his head. A story is told of the first day he attended the arithmetic class of his school, at the age of nine. Almost as soon as the teacher had finished dictating some problems, young Gauss threw down his slate with the remark, 'There it lies.' At the end of the hour, the slates were

Calculators, as above, are now widely used, even in schools. But skill in mental arithmetic was once vitally important to scientists. Sir William Hamilton, below left, and Carl Friedrich Gauss, right, were scientific geniuses, as well as mathematical prodigies. After the death of Gauss, anatomists pronounced his brain (as shown in figures 1 and 2, below), to be far more complex than that of a labourer, figures 3 and 4.

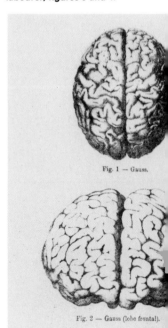

Fig. 1 — Gauss.

Fig. 2 — Gauss (lobe frontal).

checked: only Gauss' answers were correct. By the time he was 13, he was excused from further mathematics lessons; and many of his most important mathematical discoveries were made between the age of 14 and 17. He became the foremost mathematician of his age, publishing his book on the theory of numbers when he was 24. He also made notable contributions to astronomy. Throughout his life, he demonstrated an astounding ability to remember numbers and to carry out calculations in his head at uncanny speed.

MENTAL AGILITY

The multi-faceted brilliance of Hamilton and Gauss tends to obscure their extraordinary arithmetical skill. When we examine such people as Tom Fuller, Jedediah Buxton and Zacharias Dase, however, the real mystery of such strange abilities becomes evident.

Certain 18th-century African slave-dealers seem to have surprised Europeans with whom they traded by their mental agility in calculating intricate deals. However, Thomas Fuller outshone the best of them. Shipped as a slave to America, to the state of Virginia, he became known as 'the Virginia calculator'. In 1780, when he was 70, he was tested by William Hartshorne and Samuel Coates. Among the questions they asked him were the following:

'How many seconds are there in a year-and-a-half?' Fuller gave the answer in about two minutes.

'How many seconds has a man lived who is 70 years, 17 days and 12 hours old?' This time, Fuller supplied the answer in a minute-and-a-half. When his questioners told him he was wrong, he pointed out that they had not taken into account leap years. Fuller died in 1790. He had never even learned to read or write.

Another 18th-century illiterate who was nevertheless a mathematical prodigy was Jedediah Buxton, son of an English village schoolmaster. In spite of his father's occupation, Jedediah steadfastly refused to be educated, and as an adult could not even scrawl his own name. He seemed to have no interest in anything apart from calculating. In 1725, he remarked that he was drunk with reckoning. This was scarcely surprising for he had just answered, after a labour of one month (and without pen or paper) the following mammoth questions. How many barley corns, vetches, peas, beans, lentils and grains of wheat, oats and rye would fill a space of 202,680,000,360 cubic miles? And also how many hairs, each an inch long (and taking 48 hairs laid side by side to measure one inch across) would fill the same space?

His ability to solve this and similar problems earned him fame, and in 1754 he was taken to London to be examined by the Royal Society. He visited Drury Lane theatre to see Shakespeare's play *Richard III*, but his only response to this theatrical experience was to count the number of times

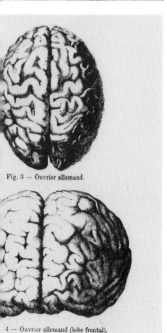

Fig. 3 — Ouvrier allemand.

4 — Ouvrier allemand (lobe frontal).

The son of a village schoolmaster, Jedediah Buxton, left, refused to learn to read and write but showed an extraordinary talent for mental computations. He excelled in very long problems that took weeks to solve, all without benefit of pen and paper. But to what extent could such an exceptional brain outdo a calculator, such as the one below?

Academy in 1837. To the question, 'What is the cubic root of 3,796,416?', the child gave the correct answer in half-a-minute. It took him less than a minute to provide the answer (which is 5) to the question, 'What satisfies the condition that its cube plus five times its square is equal to 42 times itself increased by 40?' On being asked to supply the 10th root of 282,475,249, the little boy gave the answer '7', which is correct.

The talent of an American boy, Zerah Colburn, seems to have appeared almost overnight. At first considered backward, he showed no sign of arithmetical ability at his village school. Then, one day, his father heard him reciting multiplication tables to himself without error. Soon his father was exhibiting young Colburn at various places in the United States, and took him to England in 1812. Now eight years old, Zerah was bombarded with questions such as: 'What is the square root of 106,929?' Without hesitation, he could answer '327'. To the question, 'What is the cube root of 268,336, 125?', he could give the answer '645' just as readily. He was also able to say whether a large number was a prime number. Given the number 4,294,967,297, he would even know that it was equal to 641 x 6,700,417.

Strangely, Zerah Colburn never seems to have excelled in any other activity at all; and he died at the early age of 35.

A study of such human calculators was made by an American psychologist, Dr E.W. Scripture

each actor appeared and left the stage, and the number of words each one spoke.

Another 19th-century mathematical wonder was Zacharias Dase, who was born in 1824. His extraordinary ability in mental arithmetic became evident quite early in his life; and as his fame grew, he travelled extensively throughout Europe, becoming acquainted with eminent scientists such as Gauss and the German astronomer Johann Encke. Dase seems to have had wider intellectual horizons than Buxton and Fuller, and wished to use his calculating genius in the service of mathematics and science. Since he was able to multiply and divide large numbers in his head, he was able to create mathematical tables at incredible speed. By 1847, he had calculated the natural logarithms for every number between 1 and 1,005,000 to seven figures. The length of time he required for any mental calculation was dictated by the size of the numbers involved. In one test, he multiplied together the numbers 79, 532, 853 and 93,758,479: it took him only 54 seconds. Multiplying two numbers, each of 20 figures, took him 6 minutes; two numbers, each of 40 figures, took 40 minutes; and two of 100 figures each took him 8¾ hours! All this was done without writing anything down.

A SINGULAR TALENT

Although he was anxious that his talent should be used to further the cause of science, he unfortunately had no ability beyond his gift. Many people even thought he was stupid. One teacher tried for six weeks without success to teach him the basics of mathematics. Geometry was a closed book to him. And yet in spite of all this, he did in some sense achieve his ambition. In 1849, on the recommendation of Gauss, the Hamburg Academy of Sciences gave Dase financial support to create tables of factors and prime numbers between 7 million and 10 million. He was still at this colossal task when he died in 1861.

Vito Mangiamele, son of a Sicilian shepherd, was aged 10 when he was tested by the astronomer François Arago before the French

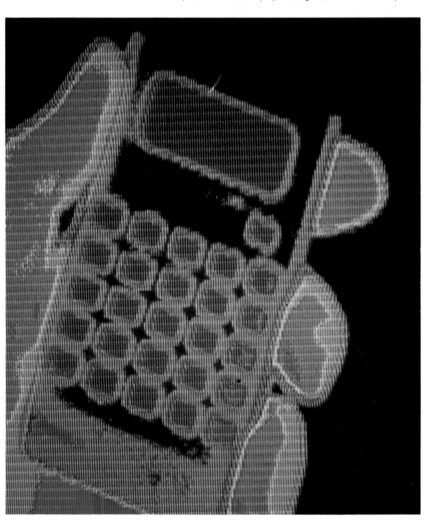

CASEBOOK

HUMAN SLIDE RULE

Born in 1806, George Bidder, *right,* was the son of an English stonemason. While still quite young, he was taken about the country by his father who wished to exhibit his son's most remarkable calculating prowess. People would test him with complicated questions such as: 'How many drops are there in a pipe of wine, if each cubic inch contains 4,685 drops and each gallon contains 231 cubic inches, and assuming there are 126 gallons in a pipe?'

Bidder was highly intelligent, and his fate was quite different from that of many other lightning calculators. He not only went to school but subsequently attended Edinburgh University, where he won the mathematical prize in 1822. Indeed, he became one of the foremost engineers in Britain, working for the Ordnance Survey and later for the Institution of Civil Engineers, of which he became president. He is regarded as the founder of the London telegraphic system and is credited with the design of the Victoria Docks in London. An expert in civil engineering in an era when England's railway system was being created, Bidder was highly sought after.

Unlike Archbishop Whately, who lost his outstanding calculating abilities at an early age, Bidder's powers actually improved as he grew older. According to a fellow of the Royal Society, he had 'an almost miraculous power of seeing, as it were; intuitively what factors would divide any large number . . . given the number 17,861, he would instantly remark it was 337 x 53.' He was not, however, able to explain how he did this.

Bidder passed on his gift to his son, George Bidder QC. Although not as brilliant a reckoner as his father, Bidder Junior became a noted mathematician who could multiply a 15 figure number by another 15 figure number in his head. Two of Bidder's granddaughters also showed considerable dexterity in mental arithmetic.

The theory that the right hemisphere of the brain (the one less used by most right-handed people) might be more active in lightning calculators was put forward in 1903 by the psychical researcher Frederic Myers. As evidence for this, he cited the fact that both Bidder QC and Edward Blyth, another 19th-century engineer and lightning calculator, were left-handed, indicating that their dominant hemisphere was the right one. However, it is not possible to determine now whether any of the earlier lightning calculators were left-handed; nor is it possible to say with certainty that the gift can be inherited.

(1864-1943), who collected accounts of many more than those described here. As a psychologist, he was naturally interested in trying to discover how such arithmetical prodigies achieve their astounding results. While his studies do not clear up the mystery completely, they do, however, throw some light on the subject.

Scripture pointed out that in order to carry out their calculations and to store a multitude of numbers in their memories for long periods of time, the lightning calculators need to have exceptional memories. Indeed, Buxton, Fuller, Dase and Colburn all gave evidence of possessing remarkable memories, often in areas other than computation. Possession of total recall would also enable the results of past calculations to be available for future operations, in much the same way that a mathematical table, once learned, is available to the ordinary mortal. Various conversion constants, such as the number of seconds in a year, or the number of inches in a mile, once assimilated, were readily available to them for future calculations.

These were fairly obvious conclusions. But Dr Scripture also suggested that other characteristics of the lightning calculator were a facility for rapid recall, a love of arithmetical computations and short-cuts, mathematical precocity and an extremely good visual imagination.

Equally curious in many ways is that aspect of the brain that enables someone to talk backwards as readily as he or she can forwards, while keeping the words of a sentence in their correct order. This

In 1981, ten-year-old Ruth Lawrence, above, *won an open scholarship to Oxford University in competition with over 500 students almost twice her age. She was assessed as possibly the most brilliant maths student ever seen in Britain.*

is a talent possessed by Andrew Levine, of the Department of Political Philosophy at the University of Wisconsin. Give him any sentence by word of mouth in any one of several languages, and he will be able to repeat it to you, with each word in reverse order, at great speed. The French sentence 'Je vais visiter ma tante la semaine prochaine', (meaning 'I am going to visit my aunt next week') thus becomes 'Ej siav retisiv am etnat al eniames eniahcorp'. Scientists believe that study of the way in which Levine and others are able to play with words in this way, or calculate at an extraordinary rate, may reveal much about brain function. Meanwhile, it has to be conceded that this particular talent serves little purpose other than to entertain.

But it should not be thought that such prodigies are exclusively male, nor that 'lightning calculators' are confined to the past. In 1981, British student Ruth Lawrence, won an open scholarship to Oxford University – at the age of ten. Many consider her to be the brightest mathematician that Oxford has ever known.

What Dr Scripture and other investigators have not yet explained is why such characteristics are found in particular individuals. If it is a question of heredity, what special constellations of genes would be necessary to create such persons? How is it that a few brains can perform supernova feats of computation that make the ordinary person's mathematical skills appear primitive? These mysteries remain as facets of the larger mystery of the human brain.

MASTERY OF FIRE

PEOPLE WHO ARE PROOF AGAINST FIRE CAN BE FOUND ALL OVER THE WORLD – ON EVERY CONTINENT AND IN EVERY KIND OF SOCIETY. WHERE DOES THE TRADITION OF 'FIRE MASTERY' HAVE ITS ROOTS? AND WHAT DOES IT MEAN TO THOSE WHO PRACTISE ITS UNLIKELY RITUALS?

George Sandwith was fascinated, like many a Westerner before him, by the fire-walking ceremonies he saw while working as a British government surveyor on the island of Suva in the Fijian group. Local adherents of one of the many Hindu sects made a practice of walking over red-hot embers, laid down in special trenches 30-40 feet (9-12 metres) long, to celebrate the feasts of local deities.

After his retirement in the 1950s, Sandwith wrote a book, *The Miracle Hunters*, in which he gave details of what he had witnessed. He also recorded the reaction of a fellow European, a banker, who was watching the phenomenon for the first time:

'Very grudgingly he admitted the fire-walking was genuine, for he had thrown something on the pit and it caught fire at once, but he was strongly of the opinion that the Government ought to stop it! When asked why, he became annoyed, replying that it does not conform with modern scientific discoveries. When I suggested that something of value might be learned from the firewalkers, he was so furious that he turned on his heel and left me.'

While the banker's 'rationalist' attitude may be understandable, it is one that has been adopted by

Jatoo Bhai, above, a 'fakir' from Calcutta, dances in the midst of a blazing fire, and will emerge unscathed. During the ritual of preparation for the firewalk, below, Jatoo Bhai goes into an attitude of prayer.

scientists in the face of such 'fire phenomena' for well over a century. More interestingly, it is paralleled by the attitudes of the leaders of those religions – Hinduism, Buddhism and Shintoism, for instance – whose followers practise 'fire-handling'. To them, such activities occupy a peripheral place at best, in relation to orthodox religion and are not in any way encouraged since they do not fit in with, and may even be contrary to, established thought.

Occasionally, an example of 'fire power' turns up in a primitive society that has no tradition of such esoteric skills, and here again the practitioner is often viewed with disapproval. The late Frank Clements, a journalist and rancher from what was then Southern Rhodesia, and who served as Mayor of Salisbury during the 1950s, gave an account of one such isolated instance that he encountered among the Shona tribe. He and a veterinary surgeon had been inoculating Shona cattle and were invited for a meal. Afterwards, squatting by the fire, Clements lit a cigarette with a Zippo lighter. As he recalled afterwards:

'It was an old one and was slightly over-fuelled, and the resulting flame was, I suppose, rather spectacular to those of the tribe who were not familiar with cigarette lighters – mostly the younger children. But there was a tribal elder present who had taken rather a dislike to my companion and me. As if showing what *he* could do, he plucked a burning brand from the fire and, holding it up to his grey-bearded face, licked the flame slowly, letting it flicker around his cheeks and nostrils. Then he quenched the flame quite deliberately between his palms, gave a snort of contempt in our direction, and tossed the stick away. He seemed to suffer no injury and his beard was not even singed.'

Jatoo Bhai works himself into a state of religious ecstasy, below, as part of the 'fireproofing' process. He then handles fire, before the dance in the flames.

Interestingly, the Shona are an agricultural people whose traditions lack any element of fire mastery – unlike, for instance, the Katanga, the BaYeke, the Mosengere and other tribes of the Congo area who are metal-working people and practise complex fire rituals and initiation rites. The Shona 'fire-eater' also appears to have been unique among his people: an individual who either had learned his skill from a wandering expert or was one of those apparently born with the gift.

Anthropologically, it is possible to trace the activities of most fire ritual societies back to a probable central source – the Iron Age shamanists of central Asia. These Tartars, Mongols and Yakuts thought of fire as one of the greatest of nature's mysteries, to be feared and revered. 'The first smith, the first shaman, and the first potter were blood brothers,' says an ancient Yakut proverb, referring to their importance in the community; but beyond doubt the smith was held in the highest esteem. He was 'master of fire' and he proved it by swallowing burning coals, walking on hot embers, and holding red-hot iron in his hands. Significantly, the greatest Tartar hero of all, Ghengis Khan, was said to have begun life as a blacksmith, and to have flown his leather apron as a battle pennant at the peak of his lance when riding to war. As a corollary to fire mastery, the smith could also endure intense cold by cultivating inner, or 'spiritual', heat, so that by overcoming both extremes of temperature he was, in the eyes of his community, super-human and on the level of a spirit or demi-god.

MASTERS OF THE FURNACE

Over the course of centuries, the knowledge and practice of fire-handling filtered out from Asia during prehistoric migrations, until about 500 BC, by when it had spread to China and Japan, Tibet and the Indian sub-continent. In Bulgaria and Greece, meanwhile, the ancient Cabiri peoples were described as 'masters of the furnace' and 'mighty in fire', for their secret knowledge eventually found its way all around the eastern Mediterranean and then down into the continent of Africa.

Fire mastery was subsequently easily absorbed into the practices of Hinduism on the Indian sub-continent. The aim of devout Hindus is to achieve the 'Brahman', or essential self, and they attempt this by following one or more of the 10 or so 'yoga' paths of self discovery. Hatha yoga, perhaps the most familiar form to Westerners, is the way to both physical control and mastery of the occult. The initiate works his way through seven stages of hatha yoga until he reaches the eighth stage, *samadhi*, which cannot be taught but is recognised by the practitioner achieving it. *Samadhi* brings with it preternatural abilities, or *siddhis*; and the men who achieve these are called *sadhus* – erroneously known to Europeans as *fakirs,* a word that properly denotes an Islamic holy man.

The majority of *sadhus* seem content to remain in one place and quietly meditate. It is the more eccentric 'fakir' types who capture the popular imagination. Some of these are genuinely sincere, setting themselves dramatic but apparently pointless tasks in their search for holiness. They may set out, for instance, to bathe in as many sacred rivers

" THE IDEA IS THAT THE SADHU TAKES ON ALL THE PAIN TO HIMSELF AND THEN NEGATES IT BY WILLPOWER ... THERE SEEMS TO BE NO RATIONAL EXPLANATION. **"**

and order the trench to be prepared and filled with hot stones. He will then lead the 'faithful' across. There are many accounts of Europeans having joined in the walks and, remarkably, few instances of serious injury. 'The idea is,' explained one commentator, 'that the *sadhu* takes on all the pain to himself and then negates it by willpower. The stones are genuinely hot, the bodies of the walkers untreated by any artificial preparation. There seems to be no rational explanation... '

FIREWALKING FEATS

Significantly, it is among the Hindu sects that the firewalkers of Polynesia, Malaya and Tahiti flourish. But the Buddhists of China, Tibet and Japan go in for almost exactly the same practices; while in Hong Kong, firewalking feats are a highly popular tourist attraction. Shintoism, the ancient nature and ancestor worship of the Japanese, also has its firewalking devotees.

E.G. Stephenson, a professor of English literature, attended a Shinto ceremony in Tokyo during which a 90-foot (27-metre) blazing trench was prepared. Professor Stephenson bravely asked if he might try. The officiating priest took him to a temple

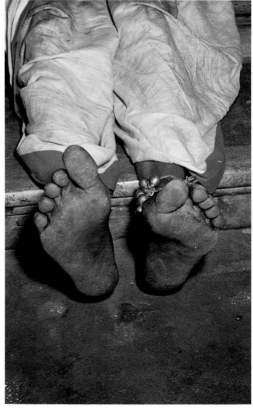

and water holes as possible, or sit motionless in a thorn bush for years until the spiky growth completely enfolds them, or permanently clench their fists so that their fingernails grow into the palms of their hands. Some, on the other hand, set out on what amounts to a deliberate circus career, and it is from among these that most of the fire masters of India are drawn. To devout and sophisticated Hindus, however, such 'showmen' are anathema, and yet the genuineness of their powers is never doubted – a contradiction that has caused a good deal of Western scepticism. It is almost as if a medieval saint were to have levitated, exhibited stigmata, and performed miracles of healing in the market place for cash.

Fire-trench walking seems to be among the most popular of the fakirs' feats. On the feast day of a local deity – there are dozens of Hindu sects and numerous gods – a fakir will arrive at a village

Jatoo Bhai dances in the flames at the climax of his ritual, above. *After the dance, the fakir displays his unburnt feet,* right, and, *equally remarkable, his unscorched clothing.*

nearby and sprinkled salt over his head, after which the professor 'strolled over the trench in quite a leisurely way', feeling only a 'faint tingling' in the soles of his feet.

There is also a strong element of showmanship about many of the voodoo rituals of the West Indies, in which fire mastery in various forms plays an important part. In Trinidad, for example, fire eaters and firewalkers abound; but it is in Haiti, where voodoo still forms the basis of most political, social and religious activity, that fire masters are most spectacular.

Dr William Sargant, author and psychiatrist, made Haitian voodoo a subject of close study for several years, coming to the conclusion that most of the phenomena take place after the participants have worked themselves into a state of deep trance. Interestingly, such voodoo practices can be traced back by way of the African Congo, Arab traders, Asia Minor and Persia to the Mongol and Tartar shamans.

INNER AND OUTER FIRE

Many West Indian slaves were exported from the Congo, among them great numbers of Yoruba. The principal god of the Yoruba tribe was Ogun, a celestial smith who taught his people to handle fire and work with metal. The Yoruba secret society, Ogboni, still has Ogun as its patron, and practises fire-handling and eating. In Haiti, meanwhile, Ogun has become Ogun Badagris, the 'bloody warrior' who demands that his followers cultivate immunity to both 'inner' and 'outer' fire.

They fulfil these requirements quite literally, firstly by dancing on live coals, and secondly by drinking prodigious quantities of fiery white rum into which ground cayenne pepper has been liberally poured. At one all-woman ceremony, Dr Sargant saw the participants not only consume this apparently lethal mixture without collapsing, but rub it into their open eyes without damaging their sight in any way. Haitian voodoo is a complex mixture of African and European influences, and Dr Sargant was interested to note that some of the women dancers wore modern welders' and metal-workers'

At the Buddhist firewalking festival 'hi watari', which is held every year at the foot of Mt Takao in Japan, the ceremony is dedicated to prayers for peace and to the health of the onlookers, who rub their ailing parts with wooden boards before throwing these on to the fire.

A Navajo fire dance, as depicted by the painter William Leigh, is shown below.

goggles, which they removed only to anoint their eyes with the rum and pepper.

The North American Indians, meanwhile, are a Mongol race in origin, their prehistoric ancestors nursed in the same Asiatic cradle as the Tartars, and carrying shamanism and its accompanying fire mastery with them from Siberia to Alaska and, from there, down the American continent. Literally every Indian tribe has at least the remnants of fire worship as part of its culture. The Canadian Hurons, for example, have retained the old skills more or less intact, as have the Apaches of the South-West and several of the Plains Indians, such as the Sioux and Cheyenne. Some tribes – the Blackfoot and Pueblo, for instance – less dramatically smear themselves with ashes, which they regard as the 'seeds of fire'.

PURIFICATION BY FIRE

Perhaps the most intriguing fire purification ceremony among North American Indians, however, is that practised by the Navajo, which combines elements of shamanism with those of the Finnish sauna. The village people prepare themselves for annual purification by building a roaring fire in the *hogan* or ritual hut. The tribe then strips naked and, led by the shaman, enters and circles the fire, while the shaman makes offerings of incense to the four quarters. A ritual dance follows, during which the women shuffle around the edge of the fire, while the men leap over and run through it. When this is over, the men and women segregate themselves, and the shaman heats long stakes of wood until they are charred and glowing. These are applied first to his own legs and then to the legs of his patients. Anyone suffering burns is considered to be in need of extra prayers. Each person then drinks a bowl of salt water, and vomits into a bowl of sand. Again, anyone who does not vomit is considered to be impure and must undergo the ritual again. Finally, the doorway of the *hogan* is sealed, and both shaman and followers sit around the fire until the flames die down and the ashes cool. These are later mixed with the vomit, taken outside and left to dry and be blown away on the wind. The purification is over for another year.

THE UNCANNY ABILITY THAT WE CALL CLAIRVOYANCE TAKES MANY FORMS, FROM A VAGUE AWARENESS OF A DISTANT EVENT TO A VIVID REVELATION. THOUGH NOT ALWAYS RELIABLE, CLAIRVOYANCE HAS SOMETIMES PROVIDED STARTLING AND UNEXPECTED CLUES IN CASES OF CRIME

CLUES FRON

In October 1978, the Los Angeles police called in a local psychic, known simply as Joan, left, to help locate a missing small boy. Convinced that he had been murdered, she provided a description of his killer, on which a police artist based his sketch, below left. In spite of certain obvious differences, the missing boy's father immediately identified it as a family acquaintance, and 'Butch' Memro, bottom, was convicted.

One day in late October 1978, seven-year-old Carl Carter disappeared from his Los Angeles home. The police were baffled: they did not know whether he had been kidnapped, or had simply wandered off and got lost.

It was then that a retired police officer suggested that a local psychic – known only by the name of Joan – might be able to help. Within hours of her involvement, the case had changed from a lost-child investigation to one of triple murder.

The psychic told the police that the boy was dead, and she even described the man she thought was responsible for his murder. Joan tried drawing his portrait, and a police artist was called in to make a more accurate sketch of the suspect, based on her description. When the drawing was shown to Carl's parents, his father said at once: 'That looks like Butch.'

Within the hour, Harold Ray 'Butch' Memro was arrested; and by the end of the day, he had confessed to strangling Carl, and to murdering two other boys two years earlier.

PSYCHIC SLEUTHS

Psychics often volunteer their services to the police, and there are countless stories of people whose extra-sensory powers have given glimpses of crimes. But all too often the accuracy of their statements cannot be verified until after the criminals have been caught by conventional means. In other words, ESP seldom leads the police directly to a culprit, as appears to have happened in the Memro case.

It has to be remembered that for every impressive case reported in the press, there are probably a hundred or more where volunteered 'psychic' help only leads the police on a wild goose chase. Following the mysterious disappearance of schoolgirl Genette Tate in August 1978, for example, the Devon police received calls from over 200 mediums and others interested in psychic detection who

SOUTH GATE
OCT 27, 78
F. G Powell

CLAIRVOYANCE

Dutch clairvoyant Gerard Croiset, seen below, has frequently assisted the police in cases concerning missing persons, including that of Pat McAdam, whose photograph he is holding.

believed their paranormal powers could produce useful clues.

The definition of clairvoyance is 'extra-sensory knowledge about material objects or events which is not obtained from another person's mind' – in other words, not simple telepathy. It can take many different forms, ranging from a vague awareness of a distant event to a vision in which scenes unfold vividly before the eyes of the clairvoyant. For ordinary people, clairvoyance is most likely to occur in stressful situations or when people or places connected with them are in danger. A well authenticated instance concerns the 18th-century Swedish scientist and seer, Emanuel Swedenborg, who was investigated by the distinguished German philosopher, Immanuel Kant. On one occasion, Swedenborg arrived in Gothenburg from England at around 4 p.m. on a Saturday. Soon he became restless and left his friends to go for a walk.

On his return, he described a vision he had experienced of a fire which, he said, had broken out just three doors away from his home, 300 miles (480 kilometres) away. A fierce blaze was raging, he said, and he continued to be disturbed until 8 p.m. when he announced that the fire had been extinguished. News of this clairvoyant vision spread rapidly through the city and Swedenborg was asked to give a first-hand account to the Governor of Gothenburg. It was not until a royal messenger arrived in Gothenburg on the following Monday that the events of Swedenborg's vision were confirmed.

Pioneer of ESP research, Dr J. Rhine, and his colleagues at Duke University, USA, decided in the 1930s to investigate clairvoyance. They had earlier conducted successful telepathy tests in which one person concentrated on a symbol while someone else, in another room, tried to read his mind. A pack of Zener cards, featuring a number of symbols, was used. The investigators at Duke University decided to see what would happen if, instead of looking at the cards, the agent simply shuffled them and then removed them one at a time from the pack, face down. The subject of the experiment had to use clairvoyance, instead of telepathy, to guess their running order. (The agent could then note down the order of the cards by going through the pack after the experiment.)

In one series of experiments in which J. Pratt was the experimenter and Hubert Pearce the subject, Pearce scored 558 correct responses out of a total of 1850 guesses. If chance alone had been at work, he should have scored only 370 correct answers. On this basis, the odds against Pearce's score were calculated as being as unlikely as 22,000 million to one.

Not everyone is impressed with laboratory results, however; and one criticism that has been levelled at the Pearce-Pratt experiments is that Pearce was unsupervised while making his guesses. Professor C.E.M. Hansel, a non-believer in ESP, has argued that, under the circumstances, the

results cannot be taken seriously. It was possible, after all, for Pearce to have sneaked out of the building after the experiment and to have peered through the window of Dr Pratt's room in order to see the cards he was turning over. He could have noted them down or memorised them, and then dashed back to his room to compile a running order with enough mistakes to make it look genuine. But another psychical researcher, Professor Ian Stevenson, has subsequently investigated the theory and has asserted that it would have been physically impossible for Pearce to have cheated in this way, since the cards would not have been visible through the window.

Even where the methodology of clairvoyant research is beyond criticism, however, the statistical nature of the results often leaves many people unimpressed. For them, individual cases of

spectacular clairvoyance are far more impressive than repeated card-guessing tests that produce staggering, above-average results.

The clairvoyance of Polish engineer Stephan Ossowiecki attracted the attention of top psychical researchers in the early 1900s. Holding a sealed envelope or a folded piece of paper, he could often describe in detail its contents or even give the name of the signatory.

During an international conference on psychical research held in Warsaw in 1923, Ossowiecki's powers were actually put to the test. An English investigator, Dr Eric Dingwall, sketched a flag with a bottle etched in its upper left-hand corner. He then wrote the date, 22 August 1923, beneath his drawing and sealed it in a package comprising three envelopes, one within the next. Dingwall sent the package from England to Baron Albert von

Important research was carried out at Duke University, USA, top, during the 1930s. The experiments used Zener cards as targets. The agent, Dr Pratt, above left, sat in either room A or room B, and withdrew cards one at a time, face down, while the subject, Hubert Pearce, above right, sat in room C and tried to name the cards as they were drawn. He was spectacularly successful, the odds against his results being 22,000 million to one.

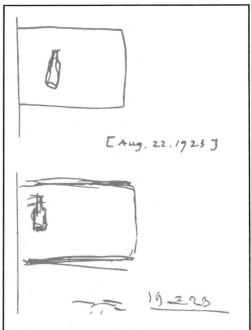

[Aug. 22. 1923]

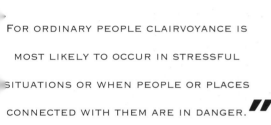

FOR ORDINARY PEOPLE CLAIRVOYANCE IS MOST LIKELY TO OCCUR IN STRESSFUL SITUATIONS OR WHEN PEOPLE OR PLACES CONNECTED WITH THEM ARE IN DANGER. **"**

Schrenck-Notzing in Warsaw. Baron von Schrenck-Notzing was a well-known pathologist of the day, and also a noted psychic investigator. Neither the Baron, nor the two other researchers involved in the experiment knew what was inside the envelope. They simply gave it to Ossowiecki without explanation and asked for his impressions.

The Polish clairvoyant told them at once that the Baron had not written the message: and that there were several envelopes, something greenish – cardboard – and a little bottle. Then he grabbed a pen and, in an agitated manner, drew an almost identical replica of the target. He also wrote '1923' and said something was written before it, but he was unable to say what this was. The test left Dingwall and the other researchers in no doubt that Ossowiecki had paranormal powers.

SECOND SIGHT

The ability to pick up impressions from objects was investigated as early as 1949 by J. Rhodes Buchanan, a physician in Ohio, USA. He found that some people he tested were able, for example, to identify medicines hidden in sealed envelopes or to give accurate descriptions of the writers of letters. He then went on to coin the word *psychometry* – which means, in Greek, 'measure of the soul' – to describe this ability.

One of the most detailed studies of clairvoyance and psychometry was carried out by a German physician, Dr Gustav Pagenstecher, who practised medicine in Mexico for 40 years. One day, a certain Maria Reyes Zierold consulted Dr Pagenstecher, complaining of insomnia. He decided to treat her by hypnosis. While in trance, she told him she could see his daughter listening at the door. To his great surprise, when he opened the door, the child was there, just as the patient had claimed. With her permission, he then set about investigating Maria Zierold's paranormal vision and soon discovered that, if an object was put in her hand while she was in trance, astonishingly, she was able to give a vivid description of events connected with it.

Once, for example, she was handed a piece of string. Immediately, she began describing a battlefield on a cold, foggy day, with groups of men and continuous rifle fire. 'Quite of a sudden,' she said, 'I see coming through the air and moving with great rapidity a big ball of fire...which drops just in the middle of the 15 men, tearing them to pieces.' The string, it transpired, had originally been attached to a German soldier's dog tag. The psychic had reported with startling accuracy a scene that the man described as 'the first great impression I received of the war'.

In an attempt to discover whether some element of telepathy was involved, or whether Maria Zierold was a genuine clairvoyant, the American Society for Psychical Research sent its research officer, Walter Prince, to conduct tests. One experiment he carried out involved two identical pieces of silk ribbon, enclosed in identical boxes. He mixed them up so that even he did not know which was which. Holding one box, Señora Zierold described a Mexican church and dancing Indians. The other gave her impressions of a French ribbon factory. She was absolutely right: one piece had come direct from the manufacturers, the other from a church altar.

With many outstanding cases of clairvoyance on record, it is not surprising to find possessors of these abilities being consulted in particularly baffling crime cases. The one consolation for criminals is that only a few outstanding clairvoyants are as spectacularly successful or as reliable as Ossowiecki or Zierold.

Winston Churchill was entertaining three of his ministers at 10 Downing Street during World War II, when he suddenly had a premonition. An air-raid had begun, but the dinner party continued without interruption, as the British Prime Minister rose and went into the kitchen where the cook and maid were working next to a high plate-glass window.

'Put dinner on a hot-plate in the dining room,' Churchill instructed the butler. Then he ordered

OBEYING THE INNER VOICE

Winston Churchill is seen, left, on one of his many visits to anti-aircraft batteries in 1941. During the Second World War, his 'inner voice' served him well; and by heeding its advice, he managed both to escape serious injury himself and to help others to do the same.

PERSPECTIVES

A STAR-STRUCK FIRST LADY

While some world leaders have based decisions purely on hunches, others in the corridors of power believe they are guided by higher forces. Nancy Reagan, wife of the former US President, Ronald Reagan, believes fervently in the value of astrology. In her early days as a Hollywood film actress, she often consulted astrologers, even attending evening astrology classes.

She found support for her occultish interests in her actor-husband, Ronald. Taking advice from an astrologer on the most propitious time for his installation as governor of California in 1967, Reagan insisted on taking the oath of office in the middle of the night – at 12.16 a.m. to be exact – while facing west.

Governor Reagan continued to show an interest in things astrological. Whenever he flew to Washington, DC, for example, he met with the well-known astrologer Jeane Dixon who repeatedly promised him that he would eventually get to occupy the White House. (The Reagans dropped Dixon when she – correctly – refused to predict Ronald as President in 1976.)

Nancy Reagan's reliance on the stars reached its zenith during her husband's presidency (1980-1988). As America's First Lady, she would secretly spend hours each week on a three-way telephone link-up with San Francisco astrologer Joan Quigley and a presidential assistant, coordinating the President's movements in and out of the White House according to a zodiac chart. If the stars predicted a good day, Reagan's appointments could be kept; if a bad day was in store, and there was a chance the President could be harmed, an alternative date would be proposed.

Sometimes, however, much to Nancy's fury, Reagan's advisers could not deter him from going out spontaneously – say, to a baseball game – when the stars advised against it. So great a trust did she have in astrology that she even had President Gorbachev's chart drawn up during the 1985 Geneva summit.

In 1987, the stars were again brought in to direct the President's schedule. After he had undergone prostate surgery in January, astrologers told Nancy that her husband should stay out of the public eye for 120 days. Said Joan Quigley: it was the 'malevolent movements of Uranus and Saturn' which 'were in Sagittarius' that kept Reagan hidden in the White House.

everyone in the kitchen to go to the bomb shelter. The Prime Minister returned to his guests and his dinner. Three minutes later, a bomb fell at the back of the house, totally destroying the kitchen.

Churchill's intuitive powers were evident throughout his life and he learned to obey them. But it was during wartime that their influence was most dramatic.

In 1941, for instance, Churchill made a habit of visiting anti-aircraft batteries during night raids. Once, having watched a gun crew in action for some time, he went back to his staff car to depart. The near-side door was opened for him because it was on that side that he always sat. But for some reason, he ignored the open door, walked round the car, opened the far-side door himself, and climbed in. Minutes later, as the car was speeding through the darkened London streets, a bomb exploded close by. The force of the blast lifted the Prime Minister's vehicle on to two wheels, and it was on the verge of rolling over when it righted itself. 'It must have been my beef on that side that pulled it down,' Churchill is said to have remarked.

Later, when his wife questioned him about the incident, Churchill at first said he did not know why he had sat on that side of the car that night. But then he added: 'Of course I know. Something said "Stop!" before I reached the car door held open for me. It then appeared to me that I was told I was meant to open the door on the other side and get in and sit there – and that is what I did'.

What the British prime minister had done was to listen to the 'inner voice' that we usually refer to as intuition or a hunch, and heed its advice. He knew

Abraham Lincoln often attended seances. At one, for instance, a piano was seen to levitate while he sat on it with his bodyguard. But his interest in the paranormal also served worthier ends, such as the Emancipation Proclamation of 1863, illustrated in A.A. Lamb's allegorical painting, above left. It is even said that Lincoln first decided to abolish slavery after a trance-lecture from a medium.

from experience that he could trust it, just as many top executives have learned to be guided by ESP in making business decisions.

PARANORMAL INFLUENCE

Other statesmen, too, have at times been guided by intuition, or have allowed the psychic talents of others to guide them. Indeed the influence of the paranormal may well have shaped the destinies of many of the world's nations.

Many believe, for instance, that American slaves owe their emancipation to the intervention of a teenager, Nettie Colburn Maynard, who gave spirit messages to Abraham Lincoln. While in trance, young Nettie is said to have lectured the President for an hour on the importance of freeing the slaves. Lincoln also attended other seances, at one of which he and his bodyguard are reported to have climbed on to a piano. Despite its load, it then lifted off the ground, until the tune being played by a medium, Mrs Miller, was finished.

When a newspaper, the Cleveland *Plain-dealer*, published a story about some of Lincoln's alleged psychic experiences, he was asked if it was true. 'The only falsehood in the statement', said the President, 'is that the half of it has not been told. This article does not begin to tell the wonderful things I have witnessed.'

The Canadian statesman
W.L. Mackenzie King, left, *often*
visited leading mediums, such as
Geraldine Cummins, above.

The pandas which Richard Nixon,
right, *took back to America in*
1972 created a huge demand for
replicas – a market that toy-maker
Herbert Raiffe had predicted the
year before.

No one knows how much the paranormal influenced the great Canadian statesman, William Lyon Mackenzie King, but his diaries certainly show that he had very distinct beliefs and was convinced that the spirits of dead politicians were in touch with him. When he visited England, he always consulted top mediums – among them Geraldine Cummins who was particularly well-known for her automatic writings.

Franklin Roosevelt also consulted a psychic – Jeane Dixon, known as the 'Washington seer'; and Nancy Reagan, of course, frequently consulted an astrologer for guidance on behalf of her husband during his presidency.

There are times, too, when ordinary citizens have premonitions about what presidents are going to do. In 1971, for example, a Brooklyn, USA, toy manufacturer, Herbert Raiffe, had a hunch that toy pandas were going to be good-sellers. There was no logic behind the decision he made. Nevertheless, he ordered that panda production should be increased severalfold at his factory.

In February of the following year, President Nixon visited China, toured the Forbidden City, and returned to America with a gift of two much-publicised pandas. No one was better placed to meet the sudden and unexpected demand for cuddly replicas than Raiffe, whose intuition seems to have tuned into an aspect of the President's China mission, long before the visit had even been arranged.

In America and Europe, the police use psychics at times to help them solve serious crimes or find missing people. Psychics have even been able to guide archaeologists to the sites of long-buried ancient remains. And around the world, the ability of dowsers to locate subterranean water supplies and other resources is well documented. So why should we find it so odd that eminent men in the political arena are also prepared to open their minds to information which comes to them in a way that by-passes normal sensory channels?

Not that it is always helpful to know what the future holds. Abraham Lincoln, for example, awoke one day, having had a vivid dream. In it, he had heard the sound of sobbing and had followed it, through the White House, until he reached a room where he found a coffin that was draped with the American flag. Lincoln, in his dream, asked a soldier who had died. 'It's the President,' came the reply. 'He has been assassinated'.

Days later, Lincoln was dead... killed by an assassin's bullet. The President's dream, it seems, had been a truly prophetic one.

Franklin Roosevelt and Winston
Churchill, above, *were both firm*
believers in the power of ESP.

BURIED ALIVE

HOW CAN A MAN – EVEN A TRAINED ADEPT, SUCH AS AN INDIAN YOGI – SUSPEND HIS BODILY FUNCTIONS IN SUCH A WAY THAT HE IS ABLE, IN EFFECT, TO SIMULATE DEATH?

It seems almost impossible to Westerners that men can deliberately put themselves in a state of suspended animation – by controlling their autonomic bodily functions, in a way not understood – and remain buried underground for hours, days, or – so it is rumoured – even years, and emerge alive. Yet, for centuries, reliable witnesses have reported many such incredible feats performed by Indian fakirs or yogis. Why, though, do they choose to engage in such an extreme form of self-mortification?

The yogi develops such disciplines to minimise inner and outer distractions in a quest for the attainment of higher consciousness. The Indian fakir, however, uses them simply to control his body rather than to reach some nebulous *samadhi*, or ecstasy. To him, live burial becomes the supreme demonstration of his power over his body and mind. But according to author and researcher Andrija Puharich, the fakir is never unconscious in the ordi-

nary sense, since one of his aims is to maintain full control of four states – waking, sleeping, dreaming and the biological shutdown of the 'false death' of catalepsy, which in the fakir's case is often self-induced. During the period of burial, he does not lose actual consciousness but enters a deep state of meditation.

Just how and why the practice first originated is lost in the mists of time, but the physician James Braid was sure of its antiquity. In his *Observations of Trance, of Human Hibernation*, he cites a passage from the *Dabistan*, a Persian classic on Indian religion: 'It is an established custom amongst the yogis that, when malady overtakes them, they bury themselves'. This implies that self-inhumation may have its origin in attitudes towards illness, and that

Among other accounts of suspended animation from Africa, mention must be made of the 'walkers for water', who were first drawn to the attention of Ivan Sanderson in 1932 by a British representative, N. H. Cleverley, in Calabar, British Cameroons. He had a senior official and a sergeant of the Native Bush Police investigate the refusal of several villages in the Ibibio tribal territory to pay their taxes. The villagers were nowhere to be found on their large swamp-surrounded islands, until the native sergeant doffed his uniform and went 'under cover'. Then he made a most startling discovery.

Peering over a 6-foot (1.8-metre) cliff, the sergeant saw 'the entire community (over a hundred souls, men, women and children, and their pets, which were confined in openwork baskets and appeared to be asleep) sitting motionless at the bottom of the water with their backs to the bank'. The sight of his sergeant shaking with fear – and failing to 'wake up' the villagers, in 8 feet (2.4 metres) of water – was too much for the European official, who fled back to Calabar. His report was not dismissed by his superiors, who were 'old Coasters' and well acquainted with the bizarre practices of the region. A second, more experienced team was dispatched; but by the time they arrived, village life was back to normal and the sergeant had collected the taxes. This was not 'a yarn', Cleverley

the technique was learned from survivors who undoubtedly reported that this extreme form of isolation hastened their cure or enhanced their ecstasies to a marked degree.

Whatever the origins of live burial, instances similar to those of India also occur in other countries where they may be associated with ritualised trance – as described in M. Eliade's *Shamanism.* In *More Things,* Ivan Sanderson tells of the burial of an unnamed fakir for 24 hours under two truckloads of gooey earth in Belize, supervised by five doctors, including a British Senior Medical Officer.

FAST DEATH

In Japan, meanwhile, there existed a strange cult of self-mummification, described in Carmen Blacker's *The Catalpa Bow.* Apparently, some Buddhists would vow to complete fasts lasting up to 4,000 days, beginning with a severely restricted diet and gradually diminishing it to a total fast with the goal of dying. At least two members of this interesting and now extinct group are recorded as entering their tombs alive.

According to the South African *Pretoria News* in late 1974, a Togolese jujuman, named Togbui Siza Aziza, was buried for three hours in Accra in an ordinary coffin. Stone slabs covered the box, then a layer of mortar, topped with more slabs. After two hours, the crowd began to panic and pleaded with Aziza, whose muffled voice could still be faintly heard. Finally, the ground shook and Aziza burst through the mortar, easily shoving the slabs aside. But the coffin was found nailed shut. Interestingly, Aziza, who subsequently toured with a group promoting African mysticism, Afrika Azzeu, said that he gained his magical powers, which include the ability to heal the sick, understand animals and be impervious to pain of any kind, by meditating while buried underground.

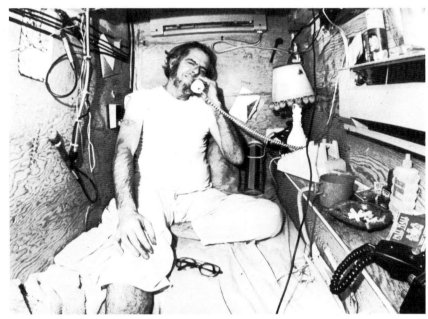

In 1974, an Indian yogi, **top,** *buried his head in earth for many long minutes, with a pulse rate of just two beats per minute, and survived. American stuntman Bill White,* **above,** *also attracted attention by staying underground for 134 days, two hours and five minutes in 1978, passing the time by telephoning the press – including the public relations officer of* **The Guinness Book of Records** *(in which he found a place).*

assured Sanderson: the incident had been soberly recorded at the court in Calabar.

This story is not unrelated to the live burial of fakirs. Either the African villagers could suspend their vital functions spontaneously, or they prevailed upon the services of some shaman skilled in techniques akin to hypnotism. But there is a record of at least one yogi who performed a very similar phenomenon by an act of his own will in Bombay, on 15 February 1950, according to a report in *The Lancet* for that year, signed by a Dr R. J. Vakil. Before a huge crowd, and under Dr Vakil's supervision, an emaciated middle-aged *sadhu* called Shri Ramdasji was sealed into a small underground cubicle for 56 hours. The chamber measured 5 by 8 feet (1.5 by 2.4 metres) and was made of concrete

studded with large nails, and plugged with more concrete. After 56 hours, a hole was bored in the lid, 1,400 gallons (6,400 litres) of water poured in through a firehose, and the hole re-sealed. The watery tomb was broken open nearly seven hours later. The *sadhu* had survived.

For 15 years after hearing the story of the Ibibio villagers, Sanderson tried to find out more. 'Trouble is,' he wrote, 'I can't find anybody in our world who will even discuss the matter sensibly and from a scientific point of view. One would have thought that this would be a golden opportunity for liars and other storytellers. Perhaps they just don't have the imagination... Perhaps, however, it is the truth...'

PERSPECTIVES

DEATH, WHEN IS THY STING?

Stephen Pile's bestselling *Book of Heroic Failures* includes 'The most unsuccessful lying in state' and 'The funeral that disturbed the corpse'. The first concerns the Bishop of Lesbos who, in 1896, after two days lying in state, suddenly sat up and demanded to know what the mourners were staring at. He was, it seems, not dead after all. In the second story, a missionary called Schwartz, who 'died' in New Delhi in the 1890s, joined in the hymn singing from his coffin during his funeral.

In the context of Pile's book, both are hilarious stories, yet premature burial was – and still is – a grim business. In the days when doctors merely felt the pulse or held a mirror to catch the mist of breath, cataleptic patients had a horrifyingly high chance of being certified dead and duly buried – alive. In primitive areas, meanwhile, knocking sounds emitting from freshly dug graves might be taken as ghostly manifestations and therefore ignored.

Such errors were most probably unintentional. But the ability to simulate death is not unknown in the West, too. St Augustine, for example, wrote of a priest who could deliberately stop his pulse and respiration during a trance state, when he was also insensitive to pain.

But, despite today's medical sophistication, the actual moment of death is a subject of hot debate. Are we 'dead' only if our hearts stop beating or when our brains cease to register electrical activity?

ELECTRIC PEOPLE

THERE ARE THOSE WHO CAN DELIVER AN ELECTRIC SHOCK WITH THEIR TOUCH, MAKE ELECTRICAL APPLIANCES STOP WORKING, OR ATTRACT OBJECTS TO THEIR BODIES. INVESTIGATIONS HAVE SHED SOME LIGHT ON THE PHENOMENON OF SUCH 'ELECTRIC PEOPLE'

Mrs Antoine Timmer went to New York with high hopes of winning a $10,000 prize offered, in 1938, for demonstrating a psychic phenomenon that could not be reproduced by trickery. The demonstration was organised by the Universal Council for Psychic Research, headed by the famous stage magician Joseph Dunninger. Mrs Timmer, seeking to understand her singular ability herself, showed how spoons and other small objects stuck to her hands and could only be removed by a vigorous tug. But her claim was dismissed because Dunninger said that he could do what she did with a concealed thread. Nonetheless, there were no allegations of trickery against

Antoine Timmer – and she no doubt went away as puzzled by her magnetic hands as she had been when she came. On their part, the Council missed a chance to explore what seemed to be a truly unexplained phenomenon.

People with unusual magnetic or electrical abilities are not all that rare. These 'human magnets' and 'human spark plugs' may attract objects to their bodies, create disturbances in electrical machines, or shock other people with their touch. But whatever their behaviour, 'electric people' still make the news at the end of the 20th century just as they did in the 19th when interest in all kinds of curiosities was particularly high.

The photograph, above, simulates the sort of discharge believed to be emitted by so-called 'human spark-plugs'.
The electric eel, above right, is an example in nature of an animal able to store and use electricity. It can deliver a shock of up to 500 volts.

1889 and concerned Frank McKinstry, of Joplin, Missouri, USA, a man with a reputation as a good dowser. He was plagued in a peculiar way: his charge was so strong in the early morning that he had to keep moving. If he stopped even for a second, he became fixed to the ground and had to wait until a helpful passer-by would be asked to pull one of his legs free.

The second case cited by Gaddis concerned 17-year-old Caroline Clare of London, Ontario, Canada, who underwent a strange undiagnosable debilitation in 1877. Her weight fell dramatically to about 6½ stone (40 kilograms), and she suffered spasms and trances. These passed after 18 months; but then the electrical phenomena began. Metal objects would jump into her hand when she reached for them and, if she held one for any length of time, it stuck to her until someone pulled if off. She shocked those she touched, in one experiment passing the shock along 20 people holding hands in a line. The electrical phenomena lasted for several months and, once gone, never returned.

The *Daily Mirror* of 2 March 1967, for example, told the story of Brian Clements, known to his friends as 'Flash Gordon' Clements, who was so highly charged that he had to discharge his voltage into metal furniture before he touched anyone. The previous week, the *Sunday Express* reported the miserable life of a certain Grace Charlesworth, who had been tormented by electric shocks in her house for a period of over two years after having lived there uneventfully for 40 years. She said: 'Sometimes they have swung me round bodily and in the night my head has started to shake as though I was using a pneumatic drill. One day sparks ran up the walls'. Curiously, it was only Mrs Charlesworth who was affected.

SHOCKING BIRTH

Not surprisingly, many instances of electric people have been noticed or recorded by doctors. In January 1869, the doctor who delivered a baby in St Urbain, France, said the infant was charged up 'like a Leyden jar' (a type of electrostatic condenser). The baby shocked all who touched him, and luminous rays emanated from his fingers. This peculiarly endowed baby had a brief life, dying in his ninth month. Douglas Hunt recorded two similar but non-fatal cases in *Prediction* magazine for January 1953. In the first instance, a doctor received a sharp shock while delivering a baby. The baby's 'electrification' lasted 24 hours, during which time he was actually used to charge a Leyden jar, and sparks issued from him. The second infant gave off a 'feeble white light' and caused 'vibrations' in small metal objects brought near his hands and feet.

Other 19th-century cases are even more spectacular. Vincent Gaddis mentions three in his book *Mysterious Fires and Lights*. The first occurred in

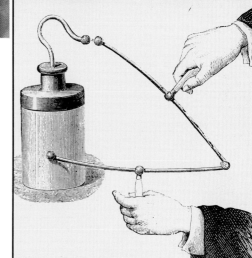

Brian Williams of Cardiff, above, **made news in 1952 as a human so full of electricity that he could light a lamp simply by rubbing it with his hand.**

The Leyden jar, right, **is a device used for storing electricity. It produces a spark when its inside and outside metal foil coatings are connected by a wire. One doctor has reported delivering a baby so 'electrified' that the child was actually used to charge a Leyden jar.**

Gaddis also mentions 16-year-old Louis Hamburger who, in 1890, was a student in Maryland, USA. When his fingertips were dry, he could pick up heavy objects simply by touching them. Pins would dangle from his open hand as though from a magnet, and only a vigorous shake would send them flying. His favourite demonstration was to place his fingers against a glass beaker full of iron filings and pull the filings up the inside of the beaker by moving his fingers on the outer surface of the container.

 THE BABY SHOCKED ALL WHO TOUCHED HIM, AND LUMINOUS RAYS EMANATED FROM HIS FINGERS ... A DOCTOR EVEN RECEIVED A SHARP SHOCK WHILE DELIVERING THIS BABY.

Both humans and animals have nervous systems that generate electricity, and some animals are able to store and use this potential. For example, electric eels – which are really fish – have an organ in their tails that produces an electric current. This current passes from the tail to the front, and enables the fish to discharge a hefty shock of up to 500 volts, depending on the animal's size and health. The biggest jolt is delivered when the fish's head and tail touch well-separated parts of the victim's body, thereby allowing the current to travel some distance. The human body can accumulate about 10,000 volts when a person walks across a thick carpet but, unlike the electric eel's shock, any jolt given is harmless. This is because the body can develop only a small electrical charge, which means in turn that the current discharged is small. In contrast to this, 'electric people' seem able to utilise their electrical potential, although they may not even want to do so. Their physiological state appears to have something to do with it, just as an electric eel's health is known to influence its electrical power.

THE DISEASE FACTOR

But what makes a person electric? According to one theory, disease may play a part – not in itself, but through its effect on the metabolism and other physiological functions. An astonishing report was made in 1920 by Dr Julius Ransom, chief physician at a state prison in New York, after 34 inmates developed a form of poisoning. During convalescence, one of them screwed up a piece of paper and tried to throw it away, but the paper stuck fast to his hand. Investigation showed that the man was carrying a high static charge, and so were all of his fellow sufferers. They found they could deflect compass needles and also make a suspended steel tape sway simply by moving their hands towards and away from it. These phenomena apparently ceased when the men recovered from their food poisoning.

There is some evidence to indicate that atmospheric and geomagnetic conditions may play a part in the strange phenomenon of electric people. Consider the case of 'a lady of great respectability', reported in the *American Journal of Science* by her physician. She was aged 30, of a nervous temperament and sedentary habits, and the wife of a prominent man in the town of Orford, New Hampshire. For two years, she had suffered from acute

Angélique Cottin, **bottom,** *was one of the most famous 'electric girls' of the 19th century. However, her powers seemed to wane when she was investigated by a hostile team appointed by the French Academy of Sciences and led by the physicist Francois Arago,* **below.** *But she was not accused of fraud.*

PERSPECTIVES
A HIGHLY-CHARGED SUBJECT

In many respects, electricity behaves like, and is described in terms of, a fluid. We speak, for instance, of an electric *current,* a stream of electrons that carry negative electric charge and are constituents of atoms. The rate of *flow* of the current is measured in amps. The 'pressure' that drives the current is electrical potential, measured in volts and more often simply called voltage. The quantity of electric charge is measured in coulombs, one coulomb being the amount of electric charge that flows when one amp passes for one second.

When electricity accumulates on the human body as a result of friction – say, of a nylon shirt rubbing on car upholstery – it may be at a potential of thousands of volts. But the quantity of charge is tiny, so that it can do little harm when discharged. This can be compared with the jet of water from a water pistol – it is delivered at a high pressure, but in too small a quantity to do any damage.

Dangerous shocks, such as those from electric mains, are caused by large currents flowing at a high voltage for a relatively long period.

Usually we are unaware of the electrical nature of matter because negative and positive charges exist in equal quantities, and their effects cancel out. Only when the two are separated are their effects seen.

Rub a plastic comb on a sleeve and it will take up electrons, which are negatively charged and can move about, from the cloth. It can then attract a small piece of paper. This is because there is a fundamental electrical law that 'likes repel, unlikes attract'. The paper's negative electrons move away and leave the surface of the paper that is closest to the comb with a surplus of positive charge. The 'positive' paper is then attracted to the 'negative' comb. There is a similar effect when a balloon is rubbed on clothing: it will gain a charge that causes it to stick to things.

rheumatism and a strange ailment called 'unseated neuralgia'. The electrical phenomena began one January evening when she was feeling distinctly odd. She happened to pass her hand over her brother's face and, as she did so, sparks shot from her fingers, to the astonishment of both. When she stood on a thick carpet, the sparks could be seen, and heard, discharging near her hands. They were brilliant and shocking, and felt not only by the woman but also by anyone she touched. The conditions favourable to bringing this about included hot weather with temperatures of about 80°F (27°C). Under these conditions, the sparks would be about 1½ inches (4 centimetres) long, coming at the rate of four a minute.

Thinking the woman's silk clothes were generating the charges, her doctor had her wear only cotton apparel. As a control, her sister wore silk. The woman's electricity was not reduced, and her sister remained normal. The electric charges, which caused her much discomfort, lasted for about six weeks, after which she was 'relieved of most of her neuralgia and other corporeal infirmities, and was in better health than she had been for many years'.

The doctor had also observed that 'a crimson aurora of uncommon splendour' was lighting the heavens and exciting scientific interest at the time of the Orford woman's strange attack. Her charges began on the same evening as this heavenly display of electricity, and the doctor felt it was no mere coincidence. Interestingly, a theory put forward by Livingston Gearhart relates instances of spontaneous human combustion to moments of change in the intensity of the Earth's magnetic field.

One of the most famous 19th-century 'electric girls' was Annie May Abbott, who toured the world as 'The Little Georgia Magnet' in the late 1880s and early 1890s. On the stage in London in 1891, she raised a chair, with a heavy man seated in it, merely by touching it with the palm of her hand. Though she weighed only 7 stone (45 kilograms), groups of men could not lift her in a chair when she resisted it. In Japan, she even overcame the attempts of the huge and skilful Sumo wrestlers to budge her from where she stood, just as she could 'neutralise' their strenuous efforts to lift any small object on which she had lightly rested her fingers. Another 'immovable' was Mary Richardson, who gave performances in Liverpool in September 1921. She was easily lifted one minute, and then six men would fail to move her even slightly. Her touch could also knock men across the stage. A.C. Holms, the Scottish psychical researcher, put his hand on Mary's shoulder while a line of 13 men pushed against her and his hand, and he felt no pressure at all from their push. He was convinced that the force exerted against her was somehow neutralised or shunted, perhaps into another dimension.

But the classic 'electric girl' must be Angélique Cottin, a 14-year-old from Normandy, France. Her ordeal began on 15 January 1846 and lasted 10 weeks. The first manifestation occurred when the weaving frame, on which she and three other girls were making gloves, twisted and rocked. Within a short time, the girl's parents exhibited her in Paris, where she came to the attention of a certain Dr Tanchou.

Dr Tanchou reported to the Academy of Sciences that the girl could identify the poles of a magnet, agitate a compass and alternately attract and repel small objects like a magnet. He also said that he could feel a sensation 'like a cold wind' in her vicinity during these activities. Objects were violently propelled away from her at her slightest touch: her bed rocked violently; chairs twisted away from under her when she tried to sit down; and a 60-pound (25-kilogram) table rose into the air when her apron brushed against it.

AN EMPTY PERFORMANCE

The Academy appointed a research team, led by the famous physicist François Arago. Although Angélique performed as best she could, the phenomena seemed to have deserted her, which also tends to happen when modern poltergeist children and 'spoon-benders' face a sceptical enquirer or the starkness of a laboratory. The committee had ignored Dr Tanchou's observations that the girl performed best when she was relaxed. Poor Angélique was extremely frightened by the situation and the manifestations that occurred, and frequently left the room. The committee reported that they could not corroborate any claims made for Angélique, but refrained from calling her a fraud.

Dr Tanchou had found that Angélique's force was strongest in the evening, especially after a meal, and that it radiated from her left wrist, inner left elbow and spine. From his experiments, Dr Tanchou believed the cause was an undiscovered form of electricity. But Arago's team was not convinced. Besides, the Academy was waging a 'holy war' against Mesmerism at the time and could not accept phenomena similar to those claimed by the detested practitioners and advocates of 'animal magnetism'. Arago recommended that the Academy treat the case of Angélique Cottin 'as never having been sent in'. And so another chance for the scientific world to discover what causes electrical phenomena in people slipped away.

TUNING IN TO TELEPATHY

IT IS SAID WE ALL ONCE HAD TELEPATHIC ABILITIES WHICH HAVE BEEN LARGELY LOST. THE EXPERIMENTS DESCRIBED HERE ARE DESIGNED BY SERENA RONEY-DOUGAL AND TEST FOR THIS HIDDEN TALENT

Imagine sitting in a comfortable chair in a darkened room, wearing headphones through which you can hear the roar of a waterfall cascading down a Welsh mountain. Your eyes are covered with halved ping-pong balls on which a red light shines, and all you can see, as you relax, is a diffuse red glow.

This extraordinary situation is part of an experiment designed to test for telepathy. As someone who has agreed to take part in the test, you are first welcomed by the experimenter, and then asked to fill in a 'mood report' describing your attitude to the experiment and your general emotional state. The experimenter then seats you in a comfortable chair, puts headphones over your ears, and, adjusts the level of waterfall noise until it is comfortable. He or she next plays another sound at such a level that you can just hear it through the waterfall noise, and then drops the noise level by five decibels so that you cannot hear it at all. The experimenter now places palmar electrodes on your left hand so that any physiological response you may experience can be monitored. Then, halved ping-pong balls are placed over your eyes, and a red light is adjusted so that it is 18 inches (45 centimetres) from your face.

The gentle waterfall sound and ping-pong eye covers should block out all external conditions and visual distractions, relaxing you into what is known as the *Ganzfeld* state. (*Ganzfeld* – from the German for 'uniform field' – refers to the unchanging or uniform level of stimulation caused by blocking external sensation.)

Finally, the waterfall sound is switched off and you are next played a tape containing the suggestion that you will now become aware of subconscious information. The waterfall sound is then switched on again.

Deprived of outside sensory stimulation, you turn mentally inwards, becoming aware of thoughts, images and memories that are the expression of your subconscious mind. At the same time, another person – the sender – begins to pass information to you by playing a tape through your headphones, so quietly that it is impossible for you to hear it against the waterfall noise. This is known as subliminal stimulation: the stimulus is physically real, but is too quiet to be perceived consciously. Instead, it is picked up at the subconscious level. The target tape, in this experiment, carries five thematically related words, and is chosen at random from four by the sender after the beginning of the experiment. Thus no one knows, for the duration of the experiment, what the tape contains.

While in this state, you are asked to voice whatever comes into your mind. What you say is recorded and, after the experiment is over, you are asked to order the sets of target words according to which of them you feel corresponds most accurately with the impressions gained while in the *Ganzfeld* state.

WORD ASSOCIATION

You now complete another mood assessment form and undergo a word association test for each of the four target tapes, in which you are presented with the four sets of five words, including the set heard subliminally, and asked to think of the individual target words, saying whatever first comes into your head. The tape of your impressions is then submitted to three independent judges, who analyse it and estimate its correspondence with the four target tapes.

In the *Ganzfeld* state, it is also possible to perceive information that is not being transmitted mechanically through the headphones, but communicated telepathically by the sender. In a separate experimental session, the sender therefore selects a tape and plays it, not through your headphones, but through *his* – at an audible level. He then tries to visualise the image that the words on the tape create, and project them mentally to you.

In the experiment, the two means of transmission – telepathic and subliminal auditory – are varied randomly. The subject therefore does not know how the information is being sent in any one session. Results show that those who are able to receive information that is transmitted subliminally are also sensitive to telepathically transmitted information; while those who find it difficult to pick up information one way generally find it equally difficult to do so in the other way. One objective of the experiments is to pinpoint the kind of psychological state – and the type of people – that make such information-transfer possible.

An analysis of one set of results showed that, out of a total of eight subjects, three consistently succeeded in identifying the target tape, placing it first or second. These three people show an awareness of the information, whether transmitted telepathically or mechanically, that is highly significant.

Transmission of information seems to require a two-stage process. The first stage involves the reception of the information in the subconscious, while the second involves forcing the subconscious knowledge into the conscious mind. Here, it seems that those who have some awareness of the way in which their subconscious minds work have an advantage: it is they who are able to translate the often quite complex and tortuous imagery of their subconscious minds into rational terms.

During one of Serena Roney-Dougal's ESP experiments, a sender, left, listens to a tape and tries to transmit the information to a subject. In another test, Serena Roney-Dougal, below, monitors the volume level of a tape while sending a subliminal message to her subject.

The subject of a telepathy test, above, sits in a state of sensory deprivation. Halved ping-pong balls cover his eyes as he listens through headphones to the sound of the Cenarth Falls in Dyfed, Wales, left. In this relaxed, so-called Ganzfeld state, he may become aware of subliminal messages transmitted to him by the sender.

In order to illustrate the complexities of translation and interpretation, we need to consider an actual example of a *Ganzfeld* session. Here, the target tape carried the five words 'sultan, Aladdin, harem, feasting, and dancing'. While in the *Ganzfeld* state, the subject made the following remarks:

'Seeing something, don't know what it is . . . crib or something – cradle, I mean; definitely a cradle in a sitting room – Middle Ages sitting room – somebody rocking this cradle dressed in Middle Ages clothes – tapestry in the back . . . mineral – either coal or some sort of stone, mineral . . . changing to pool or something . . . flashes of light . . . beansprouts . . . kitchen – copper utensils.'

The subject, in her own analysis of her impressions, understood the cradle images as being related to the harem; the flashes of light and mineral seemed related to Aladdin and his magic lamp; and the kitchen related to the feasting. Throughout the session, she felt preoccupied with food, and the

▬▬ IN CZECHOSLOVAKIA, A SERIES OF TESTS WAS MADE BETWEEN PRACTISING TELEPATHS SITUATED MANY KILOMETRES APART. THE RECEIVER WAS NOT TOLD WHEN TRANSMISSIONS WERE TO BE ATTEMPTED AND YET, AT THE PRECISE INSTANT THAT THE SENDER WAS ASKED TO IMAGINE THAT HE HAD BEEN BURIED ALIVE, THE RECEIVER HAD A CRIPPLING ATTACK OF ASTHMA. ▬▬

LYALL WATSON, THE ROMEO ERROR

cradle image occurred again later on. While there is no direct mention of an Arabian nights scene, the subject was able to tie in the thematic content of her image with the target so as to produce what is considered to be a 'hit'. Two of the three independent judges, incidentally, agreed with her analysis.

It is, of course, easy enough to see these connections when the person identifies the target. But when a person 'misses' the target, what then? Such 'misses' are generally not considered to be worthy of attention. But can we really say that telepathic or subliminal perception is operative only on those occasions when a person manages to identify the target?

Correct perception of the target, as we have seen, is a two-stage process; and one thing that has become apparent again and again during the experiments is that most 'misses' occur *not* because the information is not getting through to the subconscious, but as a result of incorrect evaluation of impressions gained while in the *Ganzfeld* state. Images that relate to the target are generally present, but the subject is unable to relate them to the words on the target tape.

PERCEPTUAL DEFENCE

On some occasions, there appears to be what might be called a low signal-to-noise ratio: the target-related imagery is present, but there is so much extraneous information – 'noise' – from the subconscious that it is extremely hard to identify subliminal or telepathic input. This 'noise' is perhaps one of the mind's principal methods of defending itself against unwanted input. The phenomenon is well-known in psychology, especially in subliminal perception research, where it is termed 'perceptual defence'. Obvious examples are simply not hearing what you do not want to hear – an ability that makes it possible for you to hold a conversation in a roomful of noisy people, or not to hear a publican calling 'time'. A further very clear example of this was provided by one subject who, in her *Ganzfeld* session, spent 10 minutes talking about how she had given up drinking. The target words were 'tavern, keg, barrel, tankard, goblet'; but she ranked this tape fourth – last – simply because, she said, it was 'too much of a coincidence'.

Most defences, however, are more subtle than this. Take a person who, according to his own estimations, scores only very slightly above chance in both telepathic and subliminal sessions. Yet his session transcripts were scored significantly *above* chance by all three independent judges. In other words, a logical, analytical assessment of his thoughts by independent observers gave statistically significant evidence of target-related imagery. During the sessions, he was 'aware' of the target inasmuch as he thought about things that were related to the target. Yet, on four occasions, he was unable, in the analysis that followed the *Ganzfeld* session, to identify the target, mainly because he chose not to use an analytical judging procedure, instead picking the target that he 'felt' was the right one. Such personal assessment proved inaccurate.

An even clearer example of the defensive process is provided by a subject whose attitude was one of disbelief in ESP. He did not believe that the

*In*FOCUS

GAMES OF TELEPATHY

The game described here is intended to reveal whether you can bring to the fore what some believe to be a natural telepathic ability, inherent in all of us, but usually lost following childhood.

It requires two players – a 'receiver' and a 'sender' – and an ordinary pack of playing cards. The aim is for the sender to look at each card, without showing it to the other player (the receiver), who has to identify whether the card is red or black. To play, proceed as follows:

1. Sit one behind the other, so that the receiver's back faces the sender.

2. The sender now shuffles the pack of cards and lifts up the top card, looking at its face. The sender should now signal that he or she is ready to transmit information by tapping the card, and then attempt mentally to send either 'red' or 'black' – depending on the colour of the card – to the receiver. One way of doing this is to close your eyes and imagine the word 'red' or 'black' somewhere around your forehead. Alternatively, try to visualise a red door, a fire engine or a British pillar-box.

3. The receiver then calls out the colour that he or she thinks the card is.

4. The sender places a tick (for a correct answer) or a cross (for a wrong one) on a sheet of paper.

A score of 26 correct answers out of 52 – the number of cards in the pack – is what you can expect according to the laws of chance. The player who scores consistently higher than the average 50/50 score is undoubtedly making use of some kind of telepathic power.

Yet, strange as it may seem, a low score is said by some also possibly to indicate the influence of the paranormal – but in a *negative* way, since the player may be unconsciously thwarting him or herself (a condition known as 'psi blocking'.) More advanced games can, of course, be attempted, and will involve the guessing of specific suits.

Smugglers are seen being attacked by customs men in the 19th-century illustration, above. In one of Serena Roney-Dougal's sessions, the target words were 'smugglers, contraband, adventure, horses, moonlight'. The subject had impressions of ice, the Titanic, Alaskan permafrost and boys in prison, the sinister character of Steerpike from Mervyn Peake's Gormenghast trilogy, right, and Albert Pierrepoint, the last English state executioner, above left. These images may appear to have only a distant connection with the target words – but the subject's word association test later revealed that he did indeed link the word 'adventure' with 'cold', and 'smugglers' with 'gallows'.

images he saw while in the *Ganzfeld* state could bear any relationship at all to the target; yet, again and again, it did. The relationship was not patently clear, as in the case of the three 'hitters' – but it was very definitely there. Although he was himself unable to pick out the target, independent judges, with some understanding of the symbolic distortions and transformations that occur in the subconscious mind, were generally able to do so.

In one typical session, the target words were 'smugglers, contraband, adventure, horses, moonlight'. In this session, the subject talked several times about ice, icebergs, the Titanic, Alaskan permafrost and so on. After the *Ganzfeld* session, his word association with the target word 'adventure' was 'cold'; his word association with 'smugglers' was 'gallows'; and, during the session, he experienced images of boys in prison, Roman soldiers, Steerpike (a character from Mervyn Peake's Gothic novel *Gormenghast)*, with a knife in his hand, cannonballs and, most significant of all, Albert Pierrepoint, England's last state executioner.

Although there is no direct connection between these images and the target words, the word associations do provide a very revealing link. And it is important to remember that in free association work such as this, where a person is attempting to gain access to material from the subconscious, the mind works in distorted and essentially symbolic ways. Thus, we should not expect to get a direct representation of the target in the *Ganzfeld* images; rather, it is *connections* that we must look for.

Only around 10 per cent of subjects talk directly about the target theme, while transcripts frequently have many rich symbolic and associational connections that are easily recognised by the independent judges – even if they are vehemently denied by the

subjects, possibly to reduce any distress at the idea of being able to perceive a target using methods not believed in. Indeed, in the case of a person whose attitude to ESP is negative, distortions and symbolism become even more complex; but the fact that it is more difficult to unravel does not necessarily mean that the subliminal or telepathic information has not been received at a subconscious level. It means merely that the 'noise' level is higher and the 'signal' more distorted. With the 'hitters', the signal is clear and the extraneous noise, very low. Such people are familiar with their own mental processes, and can usually follow the indirect ways in which target words might influence their subconscious.

By examining the differences between those subjects who consistently hit the target and those who consistently miss, we can see that two factors emerge – factors that may account for these differences. The most important is that of attitude. Thus, someone who does not believe in his or her own capacity to become aware of subliminal and telepathic information and who claims to have had no personal experience of this sort of awareness, is very likely to miss the target. On the other hand, a person who has grown up in an atmosphere in which such things are accepted may be able to learn to hit the target much of the time.

From experimentation, it appears that we all have certain latent ESP ability. One way of becoming aware of this is to enter a passive and receptive state, such as that induced by the *Ganzfeld*, thereby learning by experience how to interpret the imagery received. In this sense, such experiments can be regarded as a kind of training programme in ESP. Through it, we may eventually come to greater understanding of the processes involved.

 A POSSIBLE VIEW IS THAT THE MIND OF THE VERY YOUNG CHILD IS OPEN TO TELEPATHIC AND CLAIRVOYANT IMPRESSIONS IN A WAY THAT THE ADULT MIND (WITH ITS MEDDLING INTELLECT) SELDOM IS.

STAN GOOCH,

CREATURES FROM INNER SPACE

WITNESSING IMPOSSIBILITY

CAN SOLID OBJECTS DEMATERIALISE, ONLY TO REAPPEAR AT ANOTHER PLACE, OR PASS THROUGH OTHER OBJECTS WITHOUT DISRUPTING THEM? IT HAS BEEN SUGGESTED THAT THIS HAPPENS WHEN 'MISLAID' ITEMS INEXPLICABLY 'JUST TURN UP'

The scientist Johann Zöllner meticulously recorded his teleportation experiments with the medium Henry Slade. In one experiment, right, Zöllner sat with his thumbs pressed down on a loop of string that dangled over the edge of the table. The single knot in the loop was secured with a wax seal. After a few minutes, Slade announced that knots had been created in the string, and those shown in the illustration were found to have appeared. On another occasion, Zöllner requested that wooden rings be linked. The 'spirits' instead transferred them to the leg of a table, as shown below – a feat that should have involved dismantling the table.

O n the morning of 6 May 1878, Johann Zöllner, professor of physics and astronomy at the University of Leipzig, Germany, sat with the American medium Henry Slade in a room that had been set aside for an experiment in parapsychology. No other person was present. Zöllner held both of Slade's hands in his own on top of the card table at which they sat. After about a minute, a small circular beechwood table, standing a few feet away, began to rock to and fro, its top rising above the edge of the card table as it did so. The circular table then slid slowly towards the card table, tipped over backwards and slid beneath it.

Nothing further seemed to happen for another minute. Slade was about to consult his 'spirit controls' about what they should expect next, when Zöllner glanced under the card table to check precisely the position of the circular table – only to find that the latter had disappeared! The two men then searched the room, but found no sign of it.

UP IN THE AIR

Zöllner and Slade then resumed their places at the card table, their hands linked on its top and their legs touching, so that Slade could not make any undetected movements. After five minutes' expectant waiting, Slade saw lights in the air, as he usually did before anything paranormal occurred in his presence. Neither Zöllner nor any of his colleagues ever saw these lights when they participated in sittings with Slade. Nevertheless, Zöllner followed the path of Slade's gaze.

'As I turned my head, following Slade's gaze up to the ceiling of the room behind my back, I suddenly observed, at a height of about 5 feet [1.5 metres], the hitherto invisible table with its legs turned upwards very quickly floating down in the air upon the top of the card table.'

experimental controls). So even parapsychologists who seem willing to accept more 'reasonable' phenomena, such as ESP, join the sceptics in dismissing such tales out of hand, regarding them as tall stories for the gullible. And because these events exceed most people's 'boggle threshold' (to use a term coined by the author Renée Haynes) and cannot be reconciled with conventional physics, they have largely been ignored in parapsychology. Zöllner, certainly, was scoffed at and never taken seriously by the parapsychological establishment – for reasons that seem to have had more to do with the fantastic nature of the events than with any obscurity in his reports or shortcomings in the conditions of observation. Another contributory factor was that Slade – years later when his powers of mediumship were in decline – was declared by an investigating committee to cheat in the production of 'spirit writing' on slates.

The floating table was no mere hallucination – it gave both men a sharp crack on the head as it descended.

This sober and careful account describes what is known as teleportation – the disappearance of matter and its subsequent reappearance at the same or another place, with no known cause being involved. (Such events are also sometimes called 'disappearance-reappearance' phenomena.) A phenomenon that is presumably closely related is the passage of matter through matter – for example, the passing of an object into or out of a sealed container, or the tying and untying of knots without the use of any obvious or 'normal' means.

Such phenomena are reported from seances, experiments with certain psychokinetic (PK) agents, and in some poltergeist cases. However, they are hardly ever witnessed under 'good' conditions (that is, with parapsychologists in attendance and full

The objects inside the capsules, top, were used by researcher Julian Isaacs in experiments. They were intended to be teleported out of the container and were as small and light as possible.

The author, Julian Isaacs, is seen above, second from right, with an experimental group. In the boxes are objects that they attempted to teleport. Two boxes have been sealed with sticking plaster, on which a grid of pencil lines has been drawn. Any tampering inevitably disturbed the grid.

The pair of leather loops, left, are depicted before and after being paranormally linked. The event occurred beneath Zöllner's cupped hands, and he actually felt the loops move.

> **❞ IF THE PARALLEL UNIVERSES OF RELATIVITY ARE THE SAME AS THOSE OF QUANTUM THEORY, THE POSSIBILITY EXISTS THAT PARALLEL UNIVERSES MAY BE EXTREMELY CLOSE TO US, PERHAPS ONLY ATOMIC DIMENSIONS AWAY OR PERHAPS IN A HIGHER DIMENSION OF SPACE — AN EXTENSION INTO WHAT PHYSICISTS CALL SUPERSPACE. ❞**
>
> **FRED ALAN WOLF,**
> **PARALLEL UNIVERSES**

Spontaneous teleportation of a spanner may seem unlikely, but there was a spate of just such events in one family following participation of the parents in Julian Isaacs' metal-bending experiments. The spanner was kept hanging on a hook in a locked garden shed, left. *It was seen there in October 1982 – but thereafter went missing and could not be found anywhere, despite a thorough search of the garden and the shed. In March 1983, the spanner was found on a wardrobe,* below, *in the five-year-old daughter's room. It was now rusty, whereas it was formerly in mint condition. All in the family insisted that they had not put it there.*

Other sittings by Slade, witnessed by Zöllner, produced 'impossible' movements of objects: on many such occasions, knots were tied in loops of string, leather or even pig-gut, while Zöllner was holding them or otherwise had them under his control. A sitting that was intended to link two wooden rings did not succeed, however, but ended with the rings 'impossibly' sitting on the central leg of a circular table, the teleportation of which has already been described. This table was well out of Slade's range when the event happened, as he was sitting with Zöllner at the other table at the time. To put the rings on the leg, any human agent would have had to take the table to pieces and reassemble it.

Zöllner's work fills a number of volumes, but only a fraction of this material is available in English translation. Yet if anyone's work deserves an attempt at replication, it is certainly Zöllner's.

Just such an attempt, apparently successful, was reported in the summer of 1932 in the *Journal*

of the *American Society for Psychical Research* (ASPR). The report was written by William Button, then president of the ASPR, who was present at the eight sittings reported and who was intimately concerned with the mediumship of 'Margery' – otherwise, Margery Crandon.

In the experiments, the spirit of Margery's dead brother, Walter, ostensibly moved small objects into or out of various kinds of containers – cardboard boxes sealed with sticking plaster, locked wooden and metal boxes, among them. Poor Margery was bound to her chair with sticking plaster at her wrists and ankles; several turns of the plaster were used at each point, and it was marked with pencil lines that were designed to show whether the plaster had been taken off and rewound. When objects were teleported out of a container, the fact could be checked by shaking the container, when there would be no sound of the object bouncing around inside. Then another object might be teleported into the container – all without the container being opened.

A major problem with these experiments was that Margery's husband, Dr Crandon, was allowed to participate in many of the sittings and, in some of them, was even permitted to assist in controlling the medium's movements. The possibility of collusion cannot, therefore, be excluded. And Margery did indeed become embroiled in prolonged and bitter controversy in connection with other aspects of her physical mediumship.

INSTANT JOURNEY

More recently, another highly controversial psychic, Uri Geller, has claimed that a number of spontaneous teleportation events have happened to objects, or even people and animals, connected with him. For example, it is said that Geller suddenly arrived in the glass porch of his friend Andrija Puharich in Ossining, New York, having only a moment previously been walking in Manhattan, an hour's journey away.

The Indian mystic and religious teacher Sai Baba is the subject of a number of tales brought back by westerners who have visited him. His speciality is the materialisation of small objects from thin air; and the most usual gift is *vibhuti*, a powdery, greyish substance sometimes called 'holy ash'. Western parapsychologists who have visited him have never been allowed to impose controls. However, Karlis Osis and Erlendur Haraldsson managed to examine one of Baba's robes and found no pockets or other hiding places. Nor did it bear traces of *vibhuti* down the sleeves, which would be expected if Baba was in the habit of shaking it down into his hand. But the parapsychologists' judgement on him must remain open because he will not perform under controlled conditions.

One of the prime examples of apparent teleportation and the transport of matter through matter is the poltergeist case. In many such instances, stones or other missiles arrive apparently from nowhere, sometimes not becoming visible until they strike an object. A well-known case occurred in 1903. A geologist, W. F. Grottendieck, was conducting a survey in Sumatra. One night, he was sleeping in a hut roofed with a layer of large leaves, when he was awakened by small stones falling on and around him. Several more such showers then occurred, giving him a chance to investigate their origin. The stones seemed to come from the roof, but Grottendieck could find no gap in the overlapping leaves through which they might have arrived. They seemed to fall with unnatural slowness; and when he tried to catch them, they seemed to change direction. 'Intelligent' projectiles of this kind are not uncommon in poltergeist cases. However, they are not usually hot – whereas in this case, they were warm to the touch.

Very many cases, meanwhile, involve the mysterious disappearance of objects. There is even one account of someone who actually saw an object vanish. It happened to a Mrs Kogelnik, in London, in 1922. The Kogelnik household had been experiencing poltergeist disturbances for months, apparently centred on a maidservant. On this occasion, Mrs Kogelnik was working in the loft of the house. Her husband's account records: 'As my wife saw an axe disappearing before her eyes, she quitted the room. All this happened between 10 a.m. and 12 noon, and the light was good for observation.'

Many reasonably well-authenticated 'disappearance-reappearance' events could be cited. Indeed, there is now accumulating evidence that apparently completely ordinary people may experience minor ones fairly frequently. Replies to enquiries made by researcher Julian Isaacs even suggest strongly that teleportation may take place far more often than we would ever assume to be possible. Britain's Society for Psychical Research has woken up to this possibility and has started *Project JOTT* to try to collect a representative selection of such cases. (*JOTT* stands for 'just one of those things'.)

So, what does all this mean? A favourite answer has been that space has a fourth dimension, or possibly even more: that when objects appear and disappear in our world, they are actually moving to another dimension.

This is a perfectly reasonable hypothesis. But there are competing explanations, of course. One is the theory that objects can become invisible temporarily. But while this is consistent with certain kinds of cases, it would not explain the exit of objects from sealed boxes. And hallucination, another frequently proffered explanation, cannot

The subject above, focus of poltergeist events and apparent teleportations, seems to have been bodily teleported on occasions. Once, researcher Julian Isaacs, while at the subject's house, heard a loud thump from upstairs – the usual signal that the subject had 'gone missing'. Isaacs rushed upstairs and pulled open the lower door of the airing cupboard, seen above. There was the subject, seemingly in a dazed condition. Had he hidden himself there? In view of other, better-witnessed events centred on him, Julian Isaacs has expressed the belief that the subject's teleportations are genuine.

The little yellow idol, left, is a stone buddha belonging to a known PK agent who took part in researcher Julian Isaacs' experiments. It disappeared after he had spring-cleaned the shelves on which it normally stood. Several days later, there was a crash as the shell, seen here, fell to the floor and the buddha seemed to tumble out of it. This 'return' may well have been triggered by the psychic's thoughts, for he was watching a television programme on Buddhism at the time.

account for cases where permanent structural changes take place – such as the knots in Zöllner's loops of string. Where matter passes through matter in ordinary three-dimensional space, others suggest it may be taken apart, transported atom by atom and put together again accurately. Or the atoms involved may somehow be made 'passive' and non-cohesive, so that they do not interact with each other as the objects pass through one another.

QUANTUM TUNNELLING

A process that seems to offer an analogy on the atomic scale to the transport of matter through matter is 'quantum tunnelling', in which an atomic particle 'impossibly' breaks through an energy barrier: the particle is whimsically viewed as tunnelling its way through a barrier that is too high to be jumped. Thus, it could be that the transport of matter through matter is a large-scale quantum tunnelling phenomenon. But two daunting questions then arise. Firstly, how can the tunnelling effect, usually operative only over atomic distances, be multiplied to give the kinds of distances encountered in paranormal reports? Secondly – and this problem is common to all attempts to apply quantum theory to large-scale *psi* events – how are the billions of atoms in normal-sized objects co-ordinated to make each one simultaneously tunnel to the same place?

What is needed is determined research to find people gifted in teleportation, to train them to produce effects under good control, to catalogue the experiences of many ordinary people who also experience similar events, and to use modern electronic technology to explore the phenomenon. If a fourth dimension really exists, this opens up the stunning possibility that there may be an infinite number of other dimensions – perhaps making up an array of parallel universes. The next time you curse an object that has unaccountably disappeared a moment after you have put it down, spare a thought for the possibility that, behind this commonplace event, there may lurk fantastic realities.

Stella Lansing, *right,* a housewife from Massachusetts, found she had the ability to capture phantom forms, flashes of light or UFO-like objects on film after a close encounter in the 1960s. Following that episode, she produced well over 500 colour ciné films as well as still photographs showing strange artefacts that were not visible when the pictures were taken. Particularly interesting is the compulsion she felt to aim her camera at, say, a street scene by a sudden sensation of cold or simply a strong intuition. Psychiatrist Dr Berthold Schwarz spent several years investigating Mrs Lansing and became convinced of the genuineness of her images.

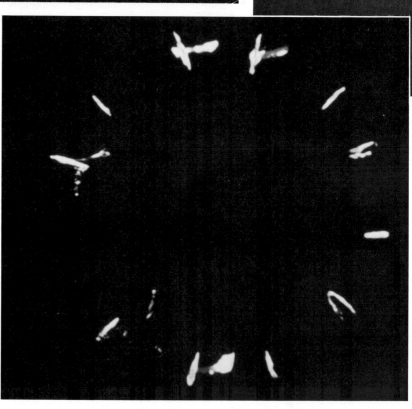

Can the camera 'see' what the human eye cannot? Spiritualists and psychics have often offered photographic 'proof' of their beliefs; but all too frequently what seemed to be paranormal effects have turned out to be the result of faulty equipment – or downright fraud. Yet, as we show, some psychic photographs, although controversial, remain essentially unexplained

London medium Gladys Hayter began to specialise in psychic photography in 1970, when she bought an Instamatic and noticed bizarre effects in her photographs – shadowy figures, swirls of light and the apparent disappearance of objects or people actually present when the photograph was taken. The fuzzy ball of light in her lap, *above,* was interpreted by her as the spirit form of a dead poodle. Sceptics have explained away her pictures as the result of a leaking camera, but a few other people also obtained odd results when they took photographs of the medium using their own equipment.

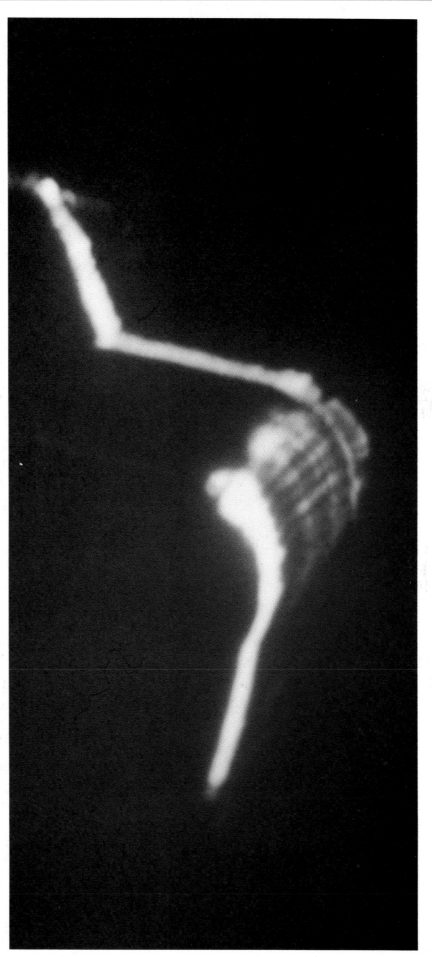

The detail, *above,* from Stella Lansing's 'clocklike' formations *left,* seems to be a classic UFO disc shape when 'frozen'. She actually saw this object as a single light moving in 'fast, erratic patterns', which appeared as this circular formation only when the *Super 8 Kodachrome* ciné film was scrutinised frame by frame. What she considered to be a 'madonna-like' figure can be seen at the top of the picture, as if moving in a fast spin from a 12 o'clock to a 1 o'clock position.

The frame from a ciné film, *right,* was taken by Stella Lansing in February 1967, and is said to show a UFO that 'took off from the knoll of a hill within a high tension line area . . . in a sudden burst of white light which, as it ascended, changed colours and then became a mere star-like flashing light... ' She considered that the leg-like protrusion that can be seen at the top of the luminescent UFO was landing-gear of some sort.

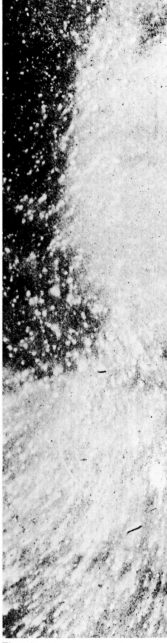

The picture, *left*, shows two UFOs, including one described by Stella Lansing as a 'Saturntype', and was taken with a *Super 8* movie camera from Route 32A near Petersham, Massachusetts, in October 1974. She described the object on the left as 'travelling on edge' and as 'coming through into our dimension'. Many such sightings apparently occurred both at night and during the day. According to Stella Lansing, the attraction is the reservoir dam and the power lines, which implies that she assumed these UFOs to be 'nuts and bolts' objects, not subjective psychic phenomena that can be seen by others only on film.

Although the mechanism behind thoughtography – the impressing of mental images on to film – remains a mystery, the phenomenon seems to exhibit marked characteristics. Typical feathery, swirling effects seen in the work of Ted Serios have also been noted in that of Charles Lancelin, as *left,* and in that of Professor Tomokichi Fukurai, as reproduced *bottom,* of the Imperial University, Tokyo, during the period between 1910 and 1913.

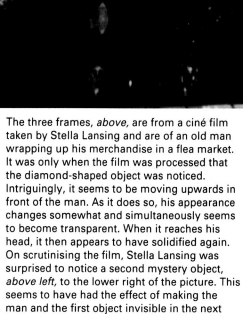

The three frames, *above,* are from a ciné film taken by Stella Lansing and are of an old man wrapping up his merchandise in a flea market. It was only when the film was processed that the diamond-shaped object was noticed. Intriguingly, it seems to be moving upwards in front of the man. As it does so, his appearance changes somewhat and simultaneously seems to become transparent. When it reaches his head, it then appears to have solidified again. On scrutinising the film, Stella Lansing was surprised to notice a second mystery object, *above left,* to the lower right of the picture. This seems to have had the effect of making the man and the first object invisible in the next frame, which appeared totally black.

The second object also then seems to have risen above the man's head and, instantly, both the first object and the man were visible once more. Stella Lansing said: 'However fantastic this may sound, I feel that there is a human image inside of the... object... ' One of the frames appears to be suffused with an amber tint, a phenomenon frequently noted by her. She could offer no straightforward explanation for her psychic films, but said: 'It's like a psychic connection with something, or someone, which causes me to grab my camera and film... Not that I hear a voice but I sense something, as though I am being controlled.'

THE MIRACLE SURGEONS

CERTAIN NATIVES OF THE PHILIPPINES AND BRAZIL ARE ALLEGEDLY ABLE TO OPERATE USING ONLY THEIR BARE HANDS. THEIR SKILL IS ENTHUSIASTICALLY PRAISED BY PATIENTS – BUT HOW DOES IT FARE UNDER SCRUTINY BY WESTERN SCIENTISTS?

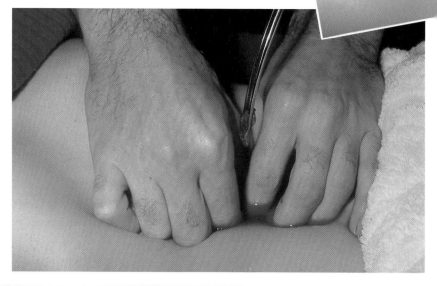

O f all paranormal phenomena, that which has become known as psychic surgery is undoubtedly one of the most extraordinary. Since the 1950s, there have been many reports of such bare-handed surgery, allegedly witnessed by scores of observers and undergone by thousands of willing patients. There is, remarkably, nothing at all furtive about the practice, and it can be seen taking place in broad daylight.

Despite extravagant claims, however, psychic surgery is now regarded by many people as no more than a shabby deception – or, more kindly, if patronisingly, as the product of primitive and super-stitious cultures. Its history seems to have followed a now familiar pattern: it looked good at first, but its credibility was soon whittled away by criticism levelled at it.

Investigators at first assured Western scientists that uneducated, medically ignorant men and

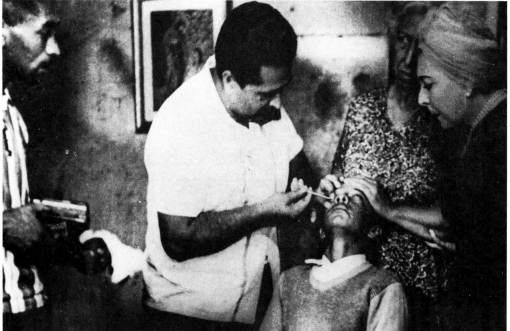

The Brazilian psychic surgeon José Pedro de Freitas, left, nicknamed Arigó, or 'yokel', is seen performing an eye operation. Arigó's surgery, often practised with such crude instruments as rusty scissors and kitchen knives, attracted a great deal of attention in the West. His operations appeared to effect genuine cures – although the work of other psychic surgeons has been laid open to doubt.

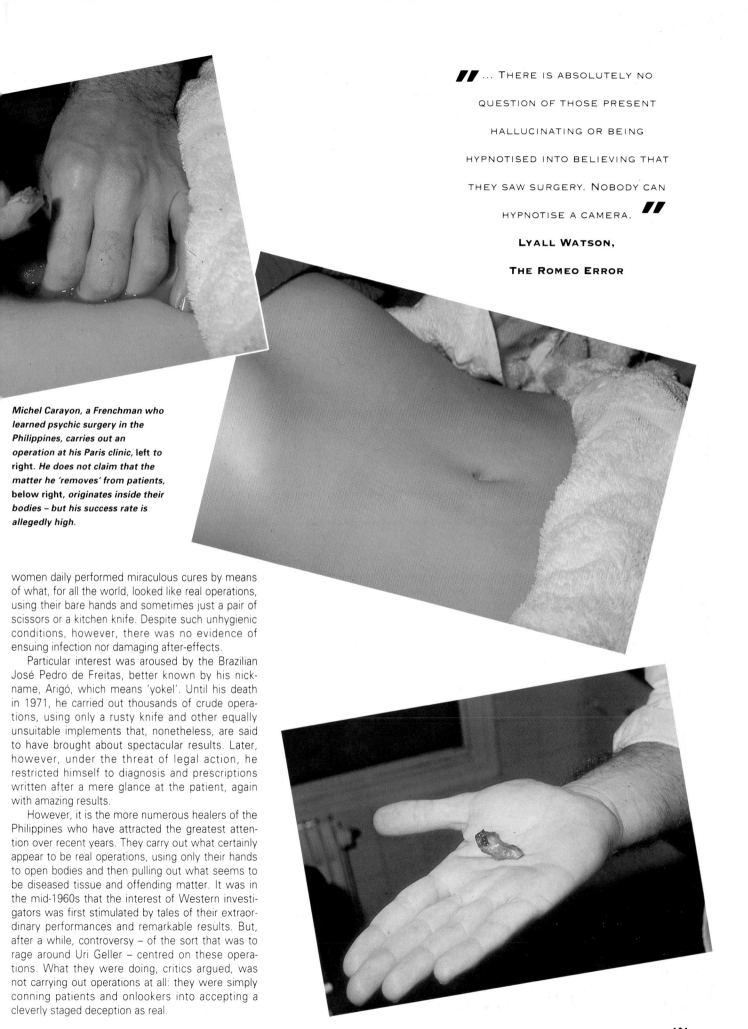

Michel Carayon, a Frenchman who learned psychic surgery in the Philippines, carries out an operation at his Paris clinic, left to right. He does not claim that the matter he 'removes' from patients, below right, originates inside their bodies – but his success rate is allegedly high.

women daily performed miraculous cures by means of what, for all the world, looked like real operations, using their bare hands and sometimes just a pair of scissors or a kitchen knife. Despite such unhygienic conditions, however, there was no evidence of ensuing infection nor damaging after-effects.

Particular interest was aroused by the Brazilian José Pedro de Freitas, better known by his nick-name, Arigó, which means 'yokel'. Until his death in 1971, he carried out thousands of crude opera-tions, using only a rusty knife and other equally unsuitable implements that, nonetheless, are said to have brought about spectacular results. Later, however, under the threat of legal action, he restricted himself to diagnosis and prescriptions written after a mere glance at the patient, again with amazing results.

However, it is the more numerous healers of the Philippines who have attracted the greatest atten-tion over recent years. They carry out what certainly appear to be real operations, using only their hands to open bodies and then pulling out what seems to be diseased tissue and offending matter. It was in the mid-1960s that the interest of Western investi-gators was first stimulated by tales of their extraor-dinary performances and remarkable results. But, after a while, controversy – of the sort that was to rage around Uri Geller – centred on these opera-tions. What they were doing, critics argued, was not carrying out operations at all: they were simply conning patients and onlookers into accepting a cleverly staged deception as real.

Evidence against the psychic surgeons then started to stack up heavily, and cries of fraud grew louder as teams of investigators began to return, not with the glowing accounts of miraculous recoveries of earlier days, but with evidence of shabby deceit and exploitation.

DAMNING EVIDENCE

In the early 1970s, debunking articles appeared first in the German press and on television. Then, in Britain, in 1975, Granada Television screened its own damning investigative programmes on psychic surgery, and these were followed in 1979 by the BBC's *Nationwide* exposé of the Elizaldes, a husband-and-wife team who visited the UK to treat patients. Yet again, what had looked like a promising, repeatable demonstration of paranormal powers in action was subjected to the same kind of public demolition.

But can the case really be said to be closed? Some are convinced that there is nothing more to be said about psychic surgery. It is simply a case of gullible observers being taken in by impressive but, in the end, identifiable sleight of hand. Is this really all that can be said? To answer these questions, first of all we need to trace the story of psychic surgery back to its roots and take a look at the evidence more closely.

The Filipino psychic surgeons were discovered among their own people, on their own territory, and within the context of their own culture and traditions. They did not ever advertise their talents, nor did they go out of their way to prove their abilities, but were tracked down by investigators from the other side of the globe.

The Philippines have a long tradition of belief in the reality of the spiritual and psychic worlds. This provided fertile ground for the Spiritist movement that took root there in the 19th century. Indeed, there are still flourishing chapters of the Spiritist society to be found throughout the Philippines. But the focal point of Spiritist activity is found on Luzon, the largest island in the archipelago, where biologist, writer and researcher Lyall Watson located the densest concentration of healers in an agricultural community 60 miles (100 kilometres) north of the capital, Manila. The majority of the healers living and working on Luzon belong to the Union Espiritista Cristiana de Filipinas, a network of rural Spiritist churches.

Lyall Watson was one of the first Westerners who went to discover for themselves what psychic surgery was all about. During three separate visits to the Philippines, occupying eight months in all, he witnessed over one thousand operations performed by 22 different healers. He was duly impressed, and what is more, he remained so despite the controversy that had already begun to detract from the credibility of earlier fulsome accounts of the Filipinos' powers.

Watson went as a scientist to carry out an unbiased investigation of the healers, and his book *The Romeo Error* tells of what he found. Also featured is a blow-by-blow account of a typical operation lasting about five minutes that, as far as Watson is concerned, was a genuine demonstration of psychic surgery.

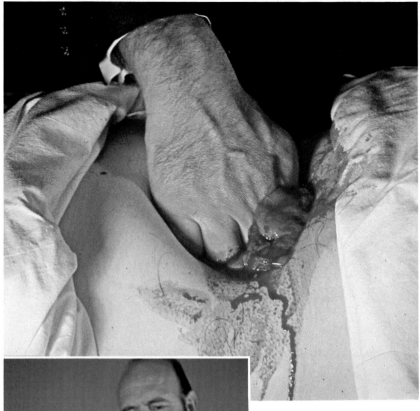

❝ WHAT FIRST STRIKES EVERYBODY WHO IS ABLE TO WITNESS PSYCHIC SURGERY IS THE AMAZING SPEED AT WHICH SOME, BUT NOT ALL, SURGEONS WORK, AND THE COMPLETE SELF-CONFIDENCE THEY ALL SHOW IN THE PROCESS. ❞

GUY PLAYFAIR, THE FLYING COW